INTERNATIONAL EXPRESS

PRE-INTERMEDIATE
Student's Book

D1511415

Liz Taylor

OXFORD UNIVERSITY PRESS

Contents

Welcome
to International Express PRE-INTERMEDIATE

Introduction	There are twelve units and three review units in this book. Each unit has four main parts: Language focus, Wordpower, Skills focus, and Social English. The unit begins with an 'agenda'. This gives you the language contents of each unit.
Language focus	First, you learn new grammar, or revise grammar you studied before. You listen to a dialogue or read a text which presents the grammar in a real-life situation. Then you study examples of the grammar to understand how to use it correctly. You think about how the grammar works and you complete the rules.

Practice
You use the grammar in different practice situations: sometimes in speaking activities, sometimes in writing exercises. The exercises help you to learn the new language and use it with confidence. You do some of the practice activities with another student or in a group.

Pronunciation
These exercises help you with pronunciation problems. You listen to examples and practise the correct pronunciation.

Wordpower	In the second part of the unit you learn new vocabulary. You also learn ways to organize and remember useful words and phrases.
Skills focus	In the third part of each unit you improve your listening, speaking, and reading skills. You listen to interviews or read longer texts and you discuss topics in pairs or groups. You also practise writing and do project work.
Social English	In the last part of each unit you learn the phrases you need for socializing with people at work or outside work. You also learn the phrases you need for telephoning in English.
Review units	There are three review units. You choose what to revise and complete the review exercises. You can use the self-check boxes to check your learning.
Pocket Book	In a pocket at the back of the Student's Book there is a separate reference book with useful language from the *International Express* Student's Book. You can use the Pocket Book in your lessons and take it with you when you travel. It has a Grammar section, with grammar tables and summaries for each unit; a Social English section, with a summary of all the phrases for socializing and telephoning; and other useful information and reference material.
Tapescripts and Answer key	The tapescripts of all the listening material and the answers to the exercises are at the back of the Student's Book. You can study these after the lesson.
Workbook	There is an *International Express* Workbook which has extra exercises on grammar, vocabulary, and social English. It has a Student's Cassette with more pronunciation and social English exercises for further practice.

Good luck with learning English.
We hope you enjoy using *International Express!*

Needs analysis

Your needs in English

Tick the boxes. Add five more situations. Compare with a partner.
When do you speak English? Why do you need English?

.... *I speak English*

- *on the phone* ☐
- *on business trips* ☐
- .... ☐
- *on holiday* ☐
- .... ☐
- *for pleasure* ☐
- .... ☐
- .... ☐

I need English ....

- *to talk to customers* ☐
- *to read professional literature* ☐
- .... ☐
- *to talk to foreign colleagues* ☐
- *to talk to suppliers* ☐
- *to write letters/ faxes/memos* ☐
- *to read newspapers/ magazines* ☐
- *on the phone* ☐

UNIT 1
First meetings

Language focus ❶ Look at the pictures. What do you think happens at Vinexpo?

❷ What information do the business cards give you?
Example *James Turner works for* Wine and Dine *magazine.*

Roberto Angelini
Consultant
Export Wine Sales
BACCHUS SpA

Via della Pergola 76
50132 Firenze

TEL: 055 53 75 866 FAX: 055 53 75 867

Monique Bresson
BRESSON TRANSLATION SERVICES

MB
OFFICES

46 Chapel St, London SW1 8QW
Tel: 0171 579 5979. Fax: 0171 579 5998
26, rue Jules Ferry, 75006 Paris
Tel: 1 - 43 45 22 49. Fax: 1 - 43 45 23 88
Via Montescalari 33, 00184 Roma
Tel: 06 - 46 58 265. Fax: 06 - 46 58 286

Wine & Dine
International Magazines Inc

James Turner
Wine Journalist

15 Honeywell Street London EC4 1DT
Tel: 0171 331 8579 Fax: 0171 331 2280

1.1 ❸ Roberto introduces Monique to James at
Vinexpo. Listen to the three conversations.
Answer the questions.
Dialogue 1
1 Does James know Monique?
2 What does Monique say to James and what
is his reply?
Dialogue 2
3 Why is Monique at Vinexpo?
4 What does she ask James?
Dialogue 3
5 Why does James want to meet Monique later?
6 When do they arrange to meet?

1.2 ❹ Listen to the conversation between Monique and James in a bar. Underline the
correct answer.
Example   What does James offer Monique?
He offers her a cup of coffee/a glass of red wine/a glass of champagne.

1 What does James do when he goes to the wine regions?	He attends sales conferences/interviews people/gives presentations.
2 How often does James travel to Italy?	He travels to Italy once a year/twice a year/two or three times a year.
3 Where does Monique live?	She lives in London/Paris/Rome.

Present Simple

Read the examples. Complete the grammar rules.

Positive

- I **have** a translation business.
- He/She **lives** in London.
- We both **write** articles on wine.

Negative

- I **don't work** for *Wine and Dine* magazine.
- James **doesn't import** wines.
- The wine producers **don't speak** French.

Questions

- **Do** Roberto and James usually **visit** Vinexpo?
- What **do** James and Roberto **write** about?
- Where **does** Monique **live**?
- **Does** Roberto often **travel** to France?

Answers

- Yes, they **do**.
- They **write** about wine.
- She **lives** in London.
- Yes, he **does**.

Note *don't = do not*   *doesn't = does not*

- Use the .... to talk about long-term situations and routine activities.

I/you/we/they

- To make the positive, use the infinitive form.
- To make the negative, use *do + not* (*don't*) + infinitive.
- To make the question, use .... + *I/you/we/they* + infinitive.

he/she/it

- The positive form always ends in ....
- To make the negative, use .... + ... (*doesn't*) + infinitive.
- To make the question, use .... + *he/she/it* + infinitive.

How do we make questions and short answers in the Present Simple?

 Pocket Book p. 2

Practice ❶ Complete the sentences using the correct form of the verbs in brackets.

Example   Roberto .... (export) wine.
Roberto exports wine.

1 Roberto .... (write) articles on wine.

2 Monique .... (not import) wine.

3 Roberto and James always .... (meet) a lot of important people in the wine business at Vinexpo.

4 Monique .... (not live) in France.

5 The Italian wine producers .... (not speak) French.

6 James often .... (travel) to France and Italy.

❷ Write the correct question word for each picture.

When?   How often?   Which?   What?   Where?   Who?

1 ....   2 ....   3 ....   4 ....   5 ....   6 *How often?*

3 Write the questions for these answers. Use the question word in brackets.

Example   He works for *Wine and Dine* magazine. (Which?)
          Which magazine does he work for?

1 They live in Dijon. (Where?)

2 He goes there three or four times a year. (How often?)

3 They meet at Vinexpo. (Where?)

4 She visits them in June. (When?)

5 They meet important people at Vinexpo. (Who?)

6 He writes about wine. (What?)

Pronunciation

Look at the questions. We say them in different ways.

a. Do you speak Italian? ➚   b. Which languages do you speak? ➘

1.3 ① Listen to the questions on the tape. Write a. ➚ or b. ➘ .

1 .... 2 .... 3 .... 4 .... 5 .... 6 .... 7 .... 8 .... 9 .... 10 ....

1.3 ② Listen to the questions again and repeat them.

③ Complete the pronunciation rule.

● In questions that begin with *do/does*, the voice goes up at the end.

● In questions that begin with question words, the voice goes .... at the end.

---

4 Work in pairs. Practise asking and answering questions.

Example   James/work for/magazine?
          Does James work for a magazine? Yes, he does.

1 Monique/speak/Italian?

2 Where/she/work?

3 James and Roberto/write/about wine?

4 James/work for/*Wine and Dine*?

5 Roberto/know/Monique?

6 James/live in Italy?

7 he/love/his work?

8 James/go/France and Italy?

9 Where/Monique's parents/live?

10 she/travel/Paris?

5 Work in two groups, A and B.

Group A   Read the Editor's letter and write five questions.

Group B   Read the Visitor profile and write five questions.

Wine and Dine

ℰditor's letter

VINEXPO SPECIAL EDITION

Duncan Ross Editor and publisher

WELCOME BACK! Vinexpo opens this week for another meeting of old and new friends in the wine and spirits business. This is a special edition of our magazine to inform you of Vinexpo events. First we want to introduce James Turner. James works from our London office and specializes in French and Italian wines. He wants to write a book about Italian wines. He often travels to all the wine-producing countries in Europe and interviews the key people in our business. He tastes and rates wines for us every year. James enjoys photography and cooking; he likes French cuisine, and he plays golf and tennis when he has time between business trips. Come and meet James and all of us on Stand 49 and enter our competition. ■

James Turner

Visitor profile: **Monique Bresson**

ONE of the special guests of the Vinexpo organizers this year is Monique Bresson. She is here as an interpreter and translator for our Italian colleagues and you can meet her on Stand 106. Ms Bresson runs a translation agency with offices in London, Paris, and Rome. She lives in London but commutes regularly to Paris. She knows a lot about the wine business because her parents have a vineyard near Dijon. Her father comes from Hungary and she speaks Hungarian and four other European languages. She enjoys skiing, horse-riding, and sailing at the weekends.

Monique Bresson

6 Read the other text and answer the other group's questions.

7 Work in pairs. Ask and answer three questions about other students.
Examples   *Does Marco speak French?*   *Yes, he does.*
                 Where does he live?   *He lives in the city centre.*

Frequency adverbs

| 0% | never | rarely | sometimes | often | usually | always | 100% |

Read these examples and complete the grammar rule.

- I'm **always** very busy.
- He isn't **usually** late.
- They **never** visit us.
- I don't **always** get up early.
- We **usually** drive to work.
- They're **never** on time.

- We write words like *always/usually/never* after the verb *to be* but .... other verbs.

---

8 Rewrite the sentences adding frequency adverbs to make true sentences.
Add three more sentences about your daily routine.

1 I get up before 6 a.m.
2 My teacher goes to bed after midnight.
3 I drive to work.
4 I am late.

5 My friend uses a computer.
6 I speak English to colleagues.
7 My boss travels on business.
8 We are early for English classes.

9 Work in pairs. Ask your partner about his/her lifestyle. In the boxes below, tick (✓) the adverbs he/she uses. Add two more questions.
Example   **Student A** *How often do you go to a disco?*
                    Student B *Sometimes.*

LEISURE SURVEY

How often do you...	never	rarely	sometimes	often
1 play a sport at weekends?				
2 go to the theatre?				
3 eat at a restaurant?				
4 travel by plane?				
5 go out with friends?				
6 visit museums?				
7 walk in the country?				
8 read a newspaper?				
9				
10				

10 Your partner is a visitor at Vinexpo. Write a short Visitor profile about him/her for the *Wine and Dine* Vinexpo Special Edition, using the information in the Leisure survey.

Personal information file. Learning vocabulary

Organizing vocabulary

It is easier to learn and remember new words if they are in groups. You can organize new vocabulary in the following ways.

1 Topic groups

Add words to the three topics *Family*, *Flat/House*, and *Jobs*.

Family

Jobs   *Flat/House*

Family	Flat/House	Jobs
husband/wife/partner	living-room	accountant
children	dining-room	manager
parent	....	....
son/.....................	bathroom	....
uncle/.....................	....	....
single/...................../divorced	garden	doctor

2 Word groups

Complete the word groups.

to live in │ a flat/.........................
│ a city/a........................./the suburbs
│ the country/a wine region

to work │ full-time
│ ....
│ flexitime

to go to work │ by bus/........................./......................../.........................
│ on foot

Match the words which go together.

go   newspapers and magazines
listen to   TV
play   to the cinema
read   music
watch   tennis

3 Word maps

Complete the word map with vocabulary from the box.

swimming   cinema   walking
photography   reading   music   tennis

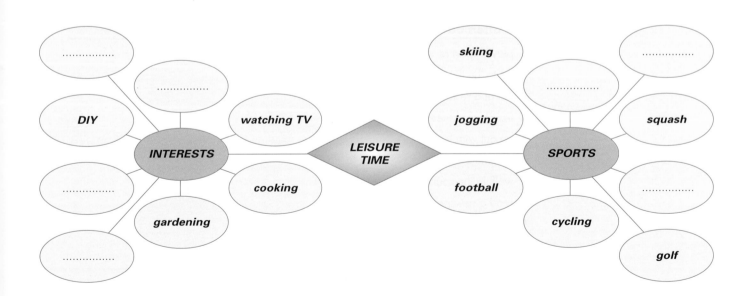

Recording meaning

When you write a new word in your vocabulary notebook or on cards, add extra information to help you remember the meaning and pronunciation.

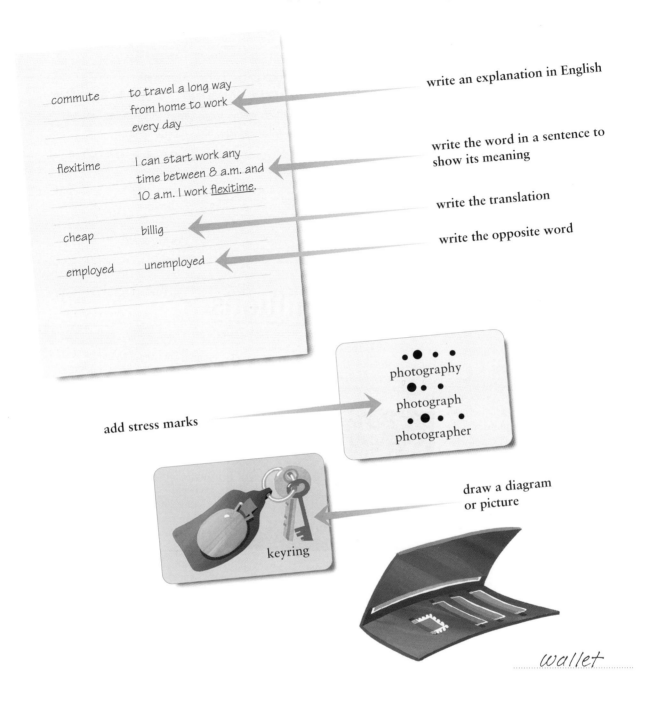

commute — to travel a long way from home to work every day

write an explanation in English

flexitime — I can start work any time between 8 a.m. and 10 a.m. I work <u>flexitime</u>.

write the word in a sentence to show its meaning

cheap — billig

write the translation

employed — unemployed

write the opposite word

photography
photograph
photographer

add stress marks

keyring

draw a diagram or picture

wallet

4 Record the meaning of the following words. Use some of the ways illustrated above.

> salary   colleague   the suburbs   a translator   a commuter   wallet   tall   large

ask for help Here are some phrases to ask for help with words. Can you add more?

Sorry, I don't understand.
Could you repeat that, please?

I don't know what ... means.
Could you speak slowly, please?

What does ... mean?
Could you spell that, please?

English: the language of millions

❶ Try to answer the questions. Then read the text to check some of your answers.

LANGUAGES QUIZ

1 Name five countries where English is the first language.

2 How many people speak English as a first language?
a. about 350 million   b. about 100 million   c. about 250 million

3 English has many words which come from other languages. Match these English words with the languages they come from.

ENGLISH WORD	LANGUAGE OF ORIGIN
umbrella	German
marmalade	Spanish
élite	Italian
quartz	French
cargo	Portuguese

English: the language of millions

Job advertisements in quality European newspapers sometimes ask for a 'good working knowledge' of English. Nowadays, large international companies often use English to communicate between offices and subsidiaries in different countries. 75% of all letters and telexes are in English and 80% of all the information in the world's computers is in English, so organizations need employees who speak good English. European professionals feel that English sometimes helps them to get a new job. It is usually a passport to more money, more travel, and more interest in their work.

Why is English so important as an international language? The statistics answer the question. About 350 million people speak English as a first language and another 300 million use English as a second

language. It is the official or semi-official language in more than 60 countries and of many international organizations. The International Olympic Committee, for

example, always holds meetings in English. Air traffic control and communication at sea around the world is always in English.

International English has a rich and

growing vocabulary. Many everyday words come from other languages. Umbrella, for example, comes from *ombra*, the Italian word for shade. English speakers get their breakfast marmalade from the Portuguese word *marmelada*. There are many Spanish words in English including cargo, flotilla, and macho; German gives the English language the words hamburger, waltz, and quartz; and French provides liaison, élite, and café.

English helps the business world to communicate across national borders. Many international companies provide language training programmes for employees. They know that English is a passport to a successful future. It is the language of millions. □

Language and International Business Journal
(Statistics from the Oxford Companion to the English Language)

❷ Work in pairs. Your company wants a new English programme. Prepare a memo for the Managing Director. Use information from the text and your own ideas.

MEMO

To: _____ Date: _____

From: _____

Subject: *English training programme*

❸ Project. Look at the list of international English words.
Tick (✓) which ones you use in your language. Find more examples.

weekend	businessman	jogging	self-service
marketing	computer	feedback	shopping
sandwich	golf	bestseller	know-how
deadline	meeting	management	jumbo jet
parking	walkman	software	smoking

Introductions, greetings, and goodbyes

1 Work in pairs. Answer the questions.

1 When do people in your country shake hands?

2 What do you say in English when you don't hear a person's name?

3 When do you say *Good morning/Good afternoon/ Good evening/Goodnight*?

2 Look at the introductions and greetings from three conversations. Underline the phrases people use when they meet someone for the *first* time.

1 Excuse me, are you...?

Hello, how are things?

May I introduce myself, I'm...

How are you?

2 Nice to see you again.   3 Let me introduce you to...

How do you do.   I'd like to introduce you to...

How's life?   Pleased to meet you.

How's the family?   Good to see you again.

1.4 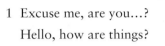 **3** Listen to the three conversations. Look at exercise 2 and tick (✓) the phrases you hear.

4 Match the phrases to the correct responses.

How are you?   Yes, that's right.

Pleased to meet you.   Then you must call me Luigi.

How do you do.   Very well, thank you. And you?

Please call me James.   How do you do.

How's life?   Pleased to meet you, too.

Hello, are you Roberto?   Not too bad, but very busy.

1.5 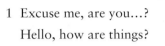 **5** Monique and James say goodbye at the airport after Vinexpo. Listen to their conversation and tick (✓) the phrases you hear.

Nice to see you again.
I must go now.
I look forward to seeing you.
It was very nice meeting you.
I really enjoyed meeting you, too.
Have a good trip back.
Thank you, and the same to you.
I hope to see you again.

6 You are in the wine business and you are at Vinexpo. Choose one of these business cards and decide why you are at the wine fair. Fill in your name in the gap on the card.

NEWSWIDE REPORT
International

NEWS PHOTOGRAPHER

VERNON MANSIONS,
WESTWAY DRIVE,
CROYDON CR9 5TL

F/A publications

Journalist

32, Belmont Square, London W1 4TQ
tel 0171 333 4656 fax 0171 367 6765

Role-play. Walk around and introduce yourself to other people in the group. Greet someone you know. Practise introducing people and saying goodbye.

UNIT 2
Professional lifestyles

Language focus ❶ Talk about one of these famous department stores or one you know.

- Harrods, in London, is the biggest department store in the UK.
- Its selling floor space is 10.5 hectares.
- It has 3,500 to 4,500 employees.

❷ Read the interview with a Harrods director about his work. Answer the questions.

1 What is the difference between a *customer*, a *buyer*, and a *supplier*?
2 What does the word *collection* mean to a fashion buyer?
3 Which employees at Harrods does Manfred see regularly?
4 Is he busy at the moment?

WHO'S WHO AT Harrods KNIGHTSBRIDGE

In our Who's Who series this month, we talk to Manfred Weiss, our new Director of Menswear, Childrenswear, and Toys. Manfred comes from Germany, and this is his third month at Harrods.

Q Manfred, you are responsible for three big departments at Harrods. How do you spend a typical day?

M Well, I have a lot of meetings. In the morning, my secretary gives me my appointments for the day, often five or six meetings with buyers. In my three departments there are fifty buyers. They visit designers and suppliers – the manufacturers of the products. They often attend fashion shows around the world looking for exciting, qual-

ity products for the store. We meet regularly to discuss ideas for our collections – the groups of new products for the next season. Generally, I don't have a lot of time for travelling. People usually bring ideas to me! I walk round my departments to talk to the sales staff and customers every day.

Q What are you working on currently?

M Well, this month, I'm having a lot of meetings with my fashion buyers. At the moment we're discussing next spring's childrenswear collections. I'm also meeting a lot of suppliers. They're coming to see me because I'm very busy at the moment and I'm not making any business trips. I'm also talking to our marketing people about sales promotions, so I have an interesting programme this month! □

③ Use the sentences below to prepare questions on the text.

Example   He has <u>five or six meetings</u>. (How many?)
How many meetings does Manfred have a day?

1 She gives him <u>his appointments for the day</u>. (What?)
2 He meets <u>groups of buyers</u>. (Who?)
3 They <u>visit suppliers</u> and <u>attend fashion shows</u>. (Who?/What?)
4 He walks round his departments <u>every day</u>. (How often?)
5 He talks to <u>the sales staff and customers</u>. (Who?)

④ Look at the text. Find one sentence about Manfred's typical day and one sentence about his work this month. What is different about the verb forms?

Present Simple and Present Continuous

Read the examples. Complete the grammar rules.

Present Simple

- I **have** five or six meetings a day.
- We **discuss** ideas for new collections.
- I **don't have** a lot of time for travelling.
- How **do** you **spend** a typical day?

Present Continuous

- This month I**'m having** a lot of meetings with buyers.
- At the moment we**'re discussing** next spring's collections.
- At present I**'m not making** any business trips.
- What **are** you **working** on currently?

- Use the .... to talk about regular activities, and the .... to talk about current activities.

- To make the ...., use *am/is/are* + *-ing* form of the verb.

How do we make short answers with the Present Continuous?

Pocket Book p. 2,3

Practice **①** Look at the sentences about Manfred and Harrods. Write (R) next to regular activities and (C) next to current activities.

1 Manfred travels to work by car every day.
2 He takes forty minutes to get to work.
3 At the moment he's talking to suppliers.
4 The sales staff usually work from 10 a.m. until 6 p.m.
5 Jeans are selling very well this season.
6 A lot of foreign visitors shop at Harrods every year.
7 Manfred isn't travelling on business this month.
8 Manfred's department is preparing for next year's collections.

② Peter Willasey also works for Harrods. Complete the description of his work. Use the Present Simple or Present Continuous form of the verbs in brackets.

Peter Willasey ....¹(work) in the Public Relations department. Every day he ....²(spend) a lot of time with foreign journalists. They often ....³ (phone) him and ....⁴(ask) for an appointment. He ....⁵(speak) to three reporters from India at the moment. He ....⁶(give) them information about Harrods for their magazines. He ....⁷(enjoy) his job very much because he ....⁸ (meet) a lot of interesting people and every day is different. Today, for example, Peter ....⁹(organize) a visit for a group of French people. They ....¹⁰(make) a film for the Louvre in Paris. They ....¹¹(film) Harrods' most famous department, the Egyptian Hall, at the moment. Newspaper and TV people often ....¹²(want) new stories on Harrods and it is Peter's job to help them.

3 Role-play. Work in pairs. You are on the telephone.
Student A Phone a company and ask to speak to someone. Use the names in the box.
Student B Explain where the person is. Use the explanations in the box. Change roles after three names.
Example **Student A** *Can I speak to Mrs Koenig, please?*
Student B *No, I'm sorry. She's not here today. She's having a meeting.*
Student A *It's very important. How about Mr Duval?*
Student B *No, I'm sorry. He's visiting our Swedish factory.*

Company staff	Explanations
Miss Adams	give/presentation to sales staff
Mr Smith	visit/our London office
Mr Kurtz	make/phone call to Paris
Mrs Li	attend/conference
Ms Engel	see/customer
Dr Brown	have/lunch with supplier

Pronunciation ① Look at the sentences. How do you pronounce the verbs?

He parks his car.   Manfred drives to work.   He finishes at six.

2.1 ② Listen to the verbs. Tick (✓) the sound you hear at the end of each word.

	/s/	/z/	/ɪz/
1 drives	....	....	....
2 visits	....	....	....
3 discusses	....	....	....
4 speaks	....	....	....
5 spends	....	....	....
6 finishes	....	....	....

2.1 ③ Listen again and repeat the verbs.

4 Work in pairs. Ask and answer questions about either Manfred or Peter using the information you have about them.
Example *Where does Manfred work?*   *He works at Harrods in London.*

5 Work in pairs. Look at the job description form. Prepare questions using the Present Simple or Continuous. Add three more questions. Ask your partner the questions and make a note of his/her answers.
Examples *When do you usually begin work?*
How often do you make business trips generally?
What projects are you working on at the moment?

JOB DESCRIPTION	NAME ....
	JOB TITLE ....

1 Working hours ....   7 Holidays ....

2 Lunch ....   8 Training courses ....

3 Meetings ....   9 Current projects ....

4 Phone calls in English ....

5 Business trips: generally ....

           this month ....   10 ....

6 Visitors: generally ....   11 ....

        this month ....   12 ....

Work file. Using dictionaries

① Read the three definitions of *work* from the *Oxford Dictionary of Business English*. Then match the sentences below with the correct definition. Write 1a, 1b, 2, or 3.

work¹ *noun*

1 (a) what a person does to earn money. (b) the place where you do this.
2 something that needs to be done. 3 the effort or energy used to produce something.

/wɜːk/

note not used with *a* or *an*. No plural and used with singular verb only.

◄► to do, find, go to, look for **work**; clerical, factory, office **work**

► labour, job, occupation, profession, trade

1 There's a lot of work to do. ....

2 She goes to work by bus. ....

3 I finish work at 5p.m. ....

4 We share an office at work. ....

5 He is looking for work. ....

6 The computer does most of the work. ....

● In this dictionary, the light blue column gives information about the grammar of the word *work* to help you use the word correctly. It also gives words which often appear with *work* (collocates), and words which have a similar meaning to *work* (synonyms).

② Read the definitions from the *Oxford Wordpower Dictionary*, and fill in the gaps with words that often appear with *job*.

☆ **job** /dʒɒb/ *noun* **1** [C] the work that you do regularly to earn money

☞ We **look for**, **apply for** or **find** a job. A job can be **well-paid/highly-paid** or **badly-paid/low-paid**. A job can be **full-time** or **part-time**, **permanent**, or **temporary**. **Job sharing** is becoming popular with people who want to work part-time. Look at the note at **work¹**.

2 [C] a task or a piece of work that may be paid or unpaid: *I always have a lot of jobs to do in the house at weekends.* ○ *The garage has done a wonderful job on our car.* **3** [C, usually sing] a function or responsibility: *It's not his job to tell us what we can and can't do.*
(IDIOMS) **do the job/trick** (*informal*) to get the result that is wanted
a good job (*informal*) a good or lucky thing: *It's a good job you reminded me – I had completely forgotten!*
the job (*informal*) exactly what is needed: *This dress will be just the job for Helen's party.*
make a bad, good, etc. job of sth to do sth badly, well, etc.
make the best of a bad job ⇨ BEST³
out of a job without paid work ☞ A more formal word is **unemployed**.
jobless *adj* (used about large numbers of people) without paid work
the jobless *noun* [plural] the people who are without work – **joblessness** *noun* [U]

to   *look for*
....

.... a job

....

full-time

....

....

He's got a .... job.

....

low-paid

Use your dictionary to look up *work* and *job*. What extra information can you find?

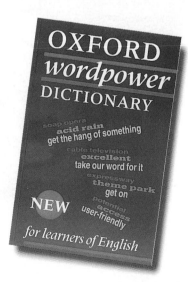

Harrods: the amazing facts

1 How do we say these numbers?

a. 100   b. 150   c. 1,000   d. 3,500
e. 20,000   f. 30,500   g. 1,000,000   h. 10,000,000

2.2 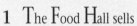 **2** Listen to an interview with Peter Willasey, Harrods' Media and Press Officer. Complete the press information sheet below.

Harrods
KNIGHTSBRIDGE
THE AMAZING FACTS

1 The Food Hall sells
   * .... different kinds of cheese.
   * .... sorts of bread and patisserie.
   * .... tons of chocolate every year.

2 The Egyptian Hall has the design and architecture of Egypt .... years ago.

3 Harrods
   * produces .... of its own electricity.
   * lights the outside of the store with .... light bulbs.
   * serves .... customers on an average day.
   * serves .... customers a day during the sales.

4 Customers spend £ .... on an average day.

5 The spending record is £ .... for the first day of the January sales.

HARRODS: Food Hall

HARRODS: Egyptian Hall

3 Work in groups. Look at the information about either IKEA or SWATCH. Prepare a short talk. Then present your talk to the other groups.

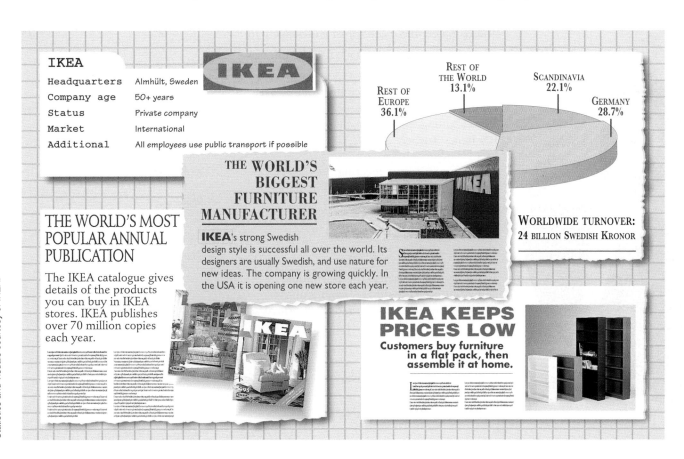

IKEA

Headquarters	Almhült, Sweden
Company age	50+ years
Status	Private company
Market	International
Additional	All employees use public transport if possible

REST OF THE WORLD 13.1%
SCANDINAVIA 22.1%
REST OF EUROPE 36.1%
GERMANY 28.7%

THE WORLD'S BIGGEST FURNITURE MANUFACTURER

IKEA's strong Swedish design style is successful all over the world. Its designers are usually Swedish, and use nature for new ideas. The company is growing quickly. In the USA it is opening one new store each year.

WORLDWIDE TURNOVER: 24 BILLION SWEDISH KRONOR

THE WORLD'S MOST POPULAR ANNUAL PUBLICATION

The IKEA catalogue gives details of the products you can buy in IKEA stores. IKEA publishes over 70 million copies each year.

IKEA KEEPS PRICES LOW

Customers buy furniture in a flat pack, then assemble it at home.

SWATCH

Headquarters	Bienne, Switzerland
Company age	12 years
Status	Public company
Market	International
Additional	Produces over 1 million watches a year

THE SWATCH PRODUCT RANGE

Watches
Mobile phones
Personal watchpagers

A New Idea in Mass Manufacture

Swatch watches – top quality at a low price. Normal watches have over 90 different parts. Swatches have only 51. But they also have the high standards of other leading Swiss brands.

COLLECTORS' SWATCHES

Swatch designs use art, music, and culture. Some are now quite valuable collectors' items.

WATCHES *to match your clothes*

Swatch designers include leading artists, architects, and industrial designers from all over the world.
Swatch produces over 200 new designs each year, so you can find one for every occasion.

4 Research project. Find out some interesting facts about your organization or any large organization that you know. Write a press information sheet or a short article about it.

Making contact

2.3 **1** James Turner is telephoning Monique Bresson at her London office. Listen to the conversation and complete the receptionist's message pad.

2.3 **2** Listen to the call again. Tick (✓) the phrases you hear.

Could I speak to Monique Bresson, please?
I'd like to speak to Monique Bresson, please.
Who's calling, please?
It's James Turner.
Hold the line, please.
I'm sorry. She's in a meeting.
I'm afraid she's busy at the moment.
Can you take a message?
Can I take a message?
Could you ask her to call me?
Could you tell her I called?

3 Work in pairs. Practise this telephone conversation. Use phrases from 2 above.
Then change roles and practise the conversation again.

Message for _____

Caller's name _____

Company _____

Number _____

Please call ☐

Caller will phone back ☐

Receptionist	Caller
Answer phone.	
	Ask to speak to Monique Bresson.
Ask who's calling.	
	Give your name and company.
Ask caller to hold the line.	
Say she's in a meeting.	
Offer to take a message.	
	Give the message.
Repeat the message.	
	Say thank you and goodbye.
Say goodbye.	

2.4  **4** James phones Monique later. Listen and complete the conversation.

R Bresson Translation Services.

J Can I _____¹ to Monique Bresson, please?

R Who's _____²?

J _____³ James Turner.

R Hold _____⁴, Mr Turner.

(*phone rings*) Monique?

M Speaking.

R I have James Turner on line 2 for you...

2.5 ⬭ **⑤** James telephones Monique another day to arrange a meeting. Listen to the phone call and tick (✓) the correct answers.

1 The appointment is with
   a. Mr Mikelore   b. Mr Michelmore   c. Mr Michinore

2 on
   a. Friday   b. Wednesday   c. Tuesday

3 at
   a. eleven o'clock   b. ten o'clock   c. three o'clock

4 His telephone number is
   a. 0171 623 5469   b. 0171 623 4459   c. 0171 623 3409

⑥ Put the letters of the alphabet in the correct columns below. Then practise saying them.

a   b   c   d   e   f   g   h   i   j   k   l   m
n   o   p   q   r   s   t   u   v   w   x   y   z

/eɪ/ (as in **say**)	/iː/ (as in **she**)	/e/ (as in **ten**)	/aɪ/ (as in **fly**)	/əʊ/ (as in **go**)	/aː/ (as in **bar**)	/uː/ (as in **who**)
a	e	f	i	o	r	u

⑦ Work in pairs. Spell your name and the names of two people in your family to your partner. Your partner writes down the names. Check the spellings are correct.

⑧ Look at these ways of saying telephone numbers.

64459   Six four four five nine   Six double four five nine
01731   Oh one seven three one (*UK*)   Zero one seven three one (*USA*)

⑨ Practise saying these numbers.

56767   293401   334477   220499   0181 23665

⑩ Work in pairs. Choose one of the letter headings below or your own company. Ask and answer questions about your companies.
Examples   *What's the name of your company?   Can you spell that, please?*
              Could you tell me your fax number, please?

PAPYRUS S.A.

rue des Grandes Filles 112
1050 Bruxelles

Tél: 02/534 93 67
Fax: 02/539 19 46

AGUASAN
Calle Castelló 75, Madrid 28006
Tel: 1 562 48 57 Fax: 1 562 98 34

HUTTON NICHOLL GOOD

Architects and Landscape Planners

The Barn House,
Chippenham, Wiltshire SN14 8EZ
TEL 01249 374226 FAX 01249 372107

UNIT 3
Business or pleasure?

Language focus **1** Which do you think are the top four tourist centres in your country? Why are they so popular?

2 Which world tourist centres do you want to visit some day? Why?

3.1 **3** Two foreign visitors are talking to a British Tourist Board interviewer after their holidays in the UK. Listen to the interview with the first visitor. Complete the form below.

Tourist Board Survey   BTB

- Name   *Massimo Reale*
- Profession
- Reason for visit to UK   *international meeting and holiday*
- Length of stay
- Places visited
- Activities
- Accommodation   *hotel in London, bed and breakfast in Scotland*

4 Read the interview with the second visitor. Complete the conversation. Use the Past Simple form of the verbs in brackets.

Interviewer So, Doctor Lebrun, you *came* (come) to London for a medical congress and for a holiday…

Dr Lebrun Yes, that's right.

Interviewer How many days *did* you *spend* (spend) in the UK?

Dr Lebrun Eight days. The congress ....¹(last) three days and after that I ....²(stay) with friends.

Interviewer Where .... you ....³(stay)?

Dr Lebrun In a hotel for the congress, and then my friends ....⁴(invite) me to stay in their London flat.

Interviewer .... you ....⁵(go) to any museums or art galleries in London?

Dr Lebrun Yes, I did. I ....⁶(spend) hours in the British Museum and the National Gallery, but I ....⁷(not visit) the Tate Gallery.

Interviewer And what .... you ....⁸(do) in the evenings?

Dr Lebrun My friends and I ....⁹(see) the musical *Cats*, and we ....¹⁰(eat) in some very good restaurants, but I ....¹¹(not have) time to go to the theatre or the opera.

Interviewer .... you ....¹²(visit) any places outside London?

Dr Lebrun Yes. We ....¹³(go) to Bath and ....¹⁴(visit) the Roman Baths and ....¹⁵(take) photos of Bath's famous architecture.

3.2 ⬜ **5** Listen to the interview and check your answers.

Past Simple

Read the examples. Complete the grammar rules.

Positive	Negative	Questions
I **stayed** with friends.	I **didn't visit** the Tate Gallery.	Where **did** you **stay?**
We **went** to Bath.	She **didn't go** to the opera.	What **did** you **do?**

Note *didn't = did not*

- Use the .... for finished situations and actions in the past.
- To make the Past Simple of regular verbs, add *-ed*.
- To make the Past Simple of irregular verbs, see Pocket Book p. 16.
- To make the negative, use .... + ... (*didn't*) + infinitive.
- To make the question, use .... + subject + ...

How do we make short answers?

Pocket Book p. 4

Practice **1** Past Simple quick test. How many words can you put in the list below?

INFINITIVE		come			find		meet		see		think	
PAST SIMPLE	ate			did	flew	found	had		said		spent		took

Pronunciation

① What's the difference in the pronunciation of *-ed* between *stayed* and *visited/lasted/attended*?

3.3 ② Listen to the verbs and tick (✓) the sound you hear at the end of each word. The first three are examples.

	stayed	walked	rented	watched	enjoyed	invited	toured	visited	talked	attended
/d/	✓									
/t/		✓								
/ɪd/			✓							

3.3 ③ Listen to the verbs again and repeat them. Complete the rule.

- In the Past Simple, when the infinitive ends in .... or ...., pronounce the *-ed* ending as /ɪd/.

2 Complete the postcard using the Past Simple form of the verbs in the box below.

> come   have   meet   visit   walk   tour   do   spend   rent   see   understand

Dear Louise

Greetings from Scotland! We ...*came*...¹ to Scotland ten days ago and ...*spent*...² a day in Edinburgh. We ...*saw did*...³ some sightseeing there and ...*visited*...⁴ the Castle, then we ...*rented*...⁵ a car and ...*saw*...⁶ the Scottish Highlands. We ...*walked*...⁷ in the mountains and ...*toured*...⁸ some beautiful places, and ...*met*...⁹ dozens of friendly local people. Sometimes we ...*didn't understand*...¹⁰ their Scottish accent! ...*did*... you ...*have*...¹¹ a good holiday last month?

Love

Anna and Massimo

3 Work in two groups, A and B.

Group A   You are interviewers for the British Tourist Board. Look at the survey form below and prepare seven questions.

Group B   Look at the information on the next page. Decide who you are and where you went last week.

Tourist Board Survey   BTB

- Name
- Profession
- Reason for visit to UK
- Length of stay
- Places visited
- Activities
- Accommodation

4 Work in pairs. Students from Group A interview students from Group B. Complete the survey form.

5 Work in groups. Ask and answer questions using the time expressions in the box.

Examples   *What did you do yesterday evening?*
            Where did you go last month?

Time expressions					
yesterday	morning afternoon evening	**last**	night weekend Sunday month summer	a week an hour two days three weeks six months a few years	**ago**

6 Write some notes to describe your last trip away from home. For a holiday, write a postcard to a friend. For a business trip, write a short report for your boss.

Holiday and travel file. Word map

1 A useful way to remember words is to make a word map. Complete the word map using the words in the box. Add more words.

hotel	coach	skiing	swimming
plane	sunbathing	museums	ferry
sightseeing	train	climbing	villa
holiday flat	tent	bed and breakfast	sailing

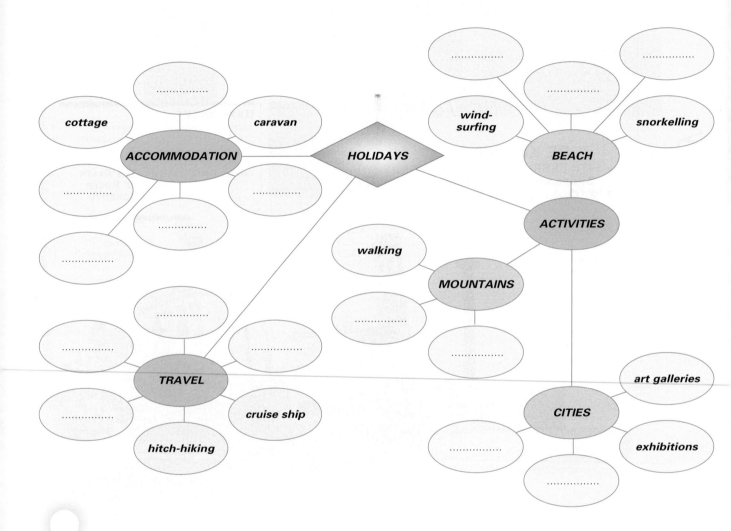

ACCOMMODATION — cottage, caravan

HOLIDAYS

BEACH — wind-surfing, snorkelling

ACTIVITIES

MOUNTAINS — walking

TRAVEL — cruise ship, hitch-hiking

CITIES — art galleries, exhibitions

2 Complete the phrases with vocabulary from the word map.

	skiing		walking		sailing
to have a	.... holiday	to do some	....	to go	....
	....		....		....
			....		....
					....

3 Make your own word map. Choose a useful topic. Use your dictionary and ask other students for new words.
Example topics *Transport/Food and drink/Sports/Leisure activities*

4 Work in pairs. Interview a partner about a recent holiday. Look at the holiday vocabulary above and ask about the type of holiday, accommodation, travel, and activities.
Examples *Where did you go?*   *How did you travel?*
What was the weather like?   *How did you spend your time?*
Did you have any problems?   *What did you enjoy most?*

Spain: a passion for life

1 Read the advertisement. Find four reasons for organizing an international conference in Spain.

You want an international meeting for *how* many people?

Spain can accommodate all kinds of business meetings: sales meetings, conferences, conventions. The country that organized the Barcelona Olympics and the Expo in Seville is ready and waiting for you.

- *Spain has a network of hotels with excellent conference facilities and communication technology*

- *and other advantages too, a wonderful climate, and great food and wines*

- *some of the best museums and art galleries in the world*

- *exciting local fiestas*

In Spain the bottom line is always the same – work and leisure in perfect harmony.

ESPAÑA

Passion for life.

Success

2 Work in two groups, A and B.

Group A Read about the Expo. Write three questions about the text.

Group B Read about the Olympic Games. Write three questions about the text.

The Expo of the Century in Seville

King Juan Carlos of Spain opened Expo '92, the largest universal exposition of the 20th century, in April 1992. It cost $285 million, and it celebrated the 500th anniversary of Christopher Columbus's discovery of America, and five centuries of scientific and technological progress.

Spain chose Cartuja Island near Seville as the location of Expo '92, and the theme *The Age of Discoveries*, because of historical links with Columbus. People believe that he spent the last ten years of his life in the beautiful monastery on the island and wrote four autobiographical books there.

With the choice of Seville for Expo '92, Spain decided on a major investment project in Andalucia. The construction work for this project took ten years and employed over 20,000 workers. It cost $7.5 billion and provided new motorways, a high-speed rail link to Madrid, and a very modern telecommunications system. Seville got new hotels and flats, a new international airport, and its first opera house, where Placido Domingo sang *Carmen* on the opening night. Seville also had the new, high-tech Cartuja Park.

Over 40 million people visited Expo '92. When it ended, it became Cartuja '93, a science, technology and cultural park, and it attracted a million visitors in the first 45 days! □

eurosport magazine

The Olympic Games with Spanish style

Spain hosted the 1992 Olympic Games with style and energy.

The Spanish won thirteen gold medals and the respect of the world for organizing this exciting and successful international event. Barcelona, already famous for its art and architecture, received $8.5 billion of public and private investment to host the Games. The city used the opportunity to improve its infrastructure. They spent $2 billion on new roads and $1 billion on the Olympic Village (housing 15,000 people), in addition to a new marina and beach facilities. Nineteen of the sports events took place in four main venues, all located within five kilometres of each other. There were over 11,000 journalists and media people, and over a million spectators at the Games. Millions more viewers watched the events on television around the world. The Olympic Games in Barcelona were a great success for the city and for Spain. ■

3 Read the other text and answer the other group's questions.

4 Discuss these questions.

1 What are the advantages and disadvantages for a country of holding world events like the World Cup, the Olympic Games, or an Expo?

2 Do you think this is the right way to spend taxpayers' money?

5 Project. Choose one of these projects.

1 Collect information about an important local event. Prepare and give a short talk about it to your group.

2 Prepare a short advertisement or TV commercial about your local region, city, or town.

Welcoming a visitor

3.4 **1** James is in California to visit a local wine business. Listen to James's conversation with the receptionist and answer the questions.

    1 Who does James want to see?   2 What does the receptionist ask him to do?

2 James is meeting Wayne Brown for the first time. Which of these topics do people often talk about when they meet professionally for the first time? Underline your choices.

the visitor's journey	the town/place they are in
the weather	other towns/cities/countries
sport	their salaries
their jobs	politics
holidays	work/jobs in general

3.5 **3** Listen to their conversation. Tick (✓) the questions Wayne asks James.

How did you get here?
Did you have any problems finding us?
Did you have a good journey?
How was your flight?
What was the weather like in London?
Is this your first visit to California?

3.6 **4** Wayne and James have lunch together and get to know each other better. What does James say about

    1 his first trip to California?   2 his career in wine journalism?

5 Which of the following do you think are important to make a good conversation? Tick (✓) your choices and add suggestions.

To be good at conversation you need to

1 listen carefully	5 answer questions and add extra information
2 give only 'yes' or 'no' answers	6 only ask questions if you are the host
3 show interest and ask questions	7 ....
4 both listen and talk	8 ....

3.6 **6** Now listen to James and Wayne again. Look at 5 above and underline what they do in their conversation. Do you think it's a good conversation? Why?

7 Here are some topics people often talk about in the first five minutes in a professional situation. Work in groups. Think of a few questions for each topic.

CONVERSATION TOPICS	
The weather	(home and away)
The visit	(travel, reason for visit)
The visitor	(family, home life, leisure, interests)
First impressions	(likes and dislikes, food and drink)
Places, travel, and holidays	(city you are in, other)
Work	(general, current projects, future plans)
Sports and leisure	(interests)
News	(local or global)

8 Now check your Pocket Book p. 18 for a list of useful questions.

Role-play. Work in pairs. One student is the host and the other student is the visitor. Choose from the topics in 7 and talk together for three minutes. Then change partners and roles.

UNIT 4
The most exciting city in the world?

▼AGENDA

▶ **Comparative and superlative adjectives**

▶ **Hotel file. Recording vocabulary with pictures**

▷ **The eighth wonder of the world**

▷ **Staying at a hotel**

Language focus ❶ Which city do you think is the most exciting in the world? Give your reasons.

❷ Work in groups. List five features which make a city good for a holiday. Compare your lists with other groups.

❸ Read the article about Sydney. Does Sydney have any of the features you listed in 2 above?

TRAVEL INTERNATIONAL

Australia's most exciting city

Sydney is a city Sydneysiders and visitors get very excited about, and it's not difficult to understand why.

IT'S the biggest, liveliest, and most cosmopolitan city in Australia. It has one of the world's loveliest harbours, and its Opera House is as famous as the Statue of Liberty. Sydney is also famous for its many beaches, where you can swim, surf, sail, and sunbathe. The nearest, Bondi Beach, is less than fifteen minutes' drive away. It's not surprising that one in five Australians chooses to live in Sydney. Few cities in the world offer a better climate, or a healthier and more enjoyable lifestyle.

The Opera House

TODAY, it's difficult to imagine the view of Sydney Harbour without the Opera House. Its adventurous design by a Danish architect won an international competition in 1957. Many people think it's the most spectacular building of this century. It took nineteen years to complete and the final cost was fifteen times more than the original estimate. Inside there are five theatres, the largest with seats for 2,700 people.

The Harbour Bridge

SYDNEY'S other famous landmark is a lot older than the Opera House. The Harbour Bridge opened in 1932. One of the best views of the harbour and the city is from the top of its south-east tower. There's an even more impressive view from the 305 metre high Sydney Tower.

The Rocks

THIS is Sydney's most historical part, where the British landed in 1788 to build the colony of New South Wales.

It has the city's oldest buildings, and its shops, museums, and pubs make it one of the most popular tourist attractions. At night, sitting at one of its waterfront cafés with the lights of Sydney Harbour all around you, it's easy to feel you're in one of the most exciting cities in the world.

4 Complete the table with adjectives from the article.

	Adjective	Comparative	Superlative
Regular	big	bigger	the ....
	....	fewer	fewest
	large	larger	....
	near	nearer	....
	old	....	....
	healthy	....	the healthiest
	lively	livelier	....
	lovely	lovelier	....
	cosmopolitan	more cosmopolitan	the ....
	enjoyable	....	most enjoyable
	exciting	more exciting	....
	impressive	....	most impressive
Irregular	good	better	the ....
	much/many	....	most
	little	....	least

Comparative and superlative adjectives

Read these examples of comparisons from the text.
Complete the grammar rules using the table above and the examples.

- Sydney's other famous landmark is a lot **older than** the Opera House.
- It cost fifteen times **more than** the original estimate.
- It's **the biggest, liveliest,** and **most cosmopolitan** city in Australia.
- Its Opera House is **as famous as** the Statue of Liberty.

One-syllable adjectives

- To make the comparative adjective, add *-er* to the end of the adjective.
- To make the superlative adjective, add *-est* to the end of the adjective.
When does the consonant double in a one-syllable adjective?

 Pocket Book p. 5

Two-syllable adjectives ending in -y

- To make the comparative, change the *-y* to *-i* and add *-er* to the end of the adjective.
- To make the superlative, change the *-y* to *-i* and add .... to the end of the adjective.

Other two-syllable adjectives and three-syllable adjectives

- To make the comparative, put *more* before the adjective.
- To make the superlative, put .... before the adjective.

Comparisons

- To compare different things, use the comparative adjective and add *than*.
How do we compare different things which are the same in some way?

 Pocket Book p. 5

Practice **1** Complete the descriptions. Use the comparative or superlative form of the adjective in brackets.

TRAVEL INTERNATIONAL

Sydney's beaches

SOUTH of Sydney, Bondi is the _____¹ (easy) beach to reach. It has the _____² (wide) range of facilities but at weekends it's _____³(crowded) and _____⁴(noisy) than the other beaches. South of Bondi, Tamarama is one of Sydney's _____⁵(beautiful) beaches, but also one of the _____⁶(dangerous) for swimming. For children, Coogee Beach is both _____⁷(safe) and _____⁸(suitable) than Tamarama.

There are several beaches north of Sydney. Manly is the _____⁹(accessible) and the _____¹⁰ (good) for surfing. Palm Beach is _____¹¹(far) from Sydney than Manly, and it takes _____¹² (long) to get to, so it's not surprising that it's _____¹³(peaceful) than the others.

Hunter Valley

A tour of Hunter Valley is one of the _____¹⁴ (popular) excursions from Sydney. It's Australia's _____¹⁵(old) wine-growing area and it produces some of the country's _____¹⁶(fine) wines. Its white wines are _____¹⁷(famous) than its red wines, but some of its red wines are very good, too. The _____¹⁸(good) time to visit Hunter Valley is during the week, when there are _____¹⁹(few) people than at weekends and accommodation is _____²⁰(cheap). The _____²¹(exciting) way to see Hunter Valley is to take a champagne balloon flight. Unfortunately, it's also the _____²²(expensive) way to see it! ■

① Listen to the examples and look at the stress patterns.

4.1 🎧 •• • • • •
a. suitable   b. expensive

4.2 🎧 ② Listen to the words on the tape. What is the stress pattern? Write a. or b.

• • • •
Example   *excitement*   *b.*

1 popular   __   3 dangerous   __   5 exciting   __
2 surprising   __   4 impressive   __   6 beautiful   __

4.2 🎧 ③ Listen again and say each word three times quietly to yourself.

④ Look at these words. What is the stress pattern? Write a. or b.

1 producer   __   3 customer   __   5 translator   __
2 consultant   __   4 quality   __   6 telephone   __

4.3 🎧 ⑤ Listen and check your answers.

---

❷ Work in pairs. Compare Australia, Canada, and the USA, using the facts in the table. Use the comparative or superlative form of the adjectives in the box.
Example   *Washington has a lower population than Ottawa.*

big	high	low	many	small

	Australia	**Canada**	**USA**
Area (sq. km.)	7.6 million	9.9 million	9.3 million
Population	17.3 million	26.8 million	252.0 million
Population of capital	250,000 (Canberra)	819,263 (Ottawa)	606,900 (Washington DC)

Source: *The Economist Pocket World in Figures 1994*

❸ Think of a city you know well. Describe it to your class but don't give the name. Compare it to Sydney. The class must try to guess the city.

❹ Work in pairs. Prepare questions for the city survey below. Add two extra questions. Ask your partner the questions and make a note of the answers.
Example   **Student A** *Which city do you think has the best climate?*
         Student B *San Francisco.*

City Survey

PARTNER'S ANSWERS

1 climate?
2 cosmopolitan?
3 interesting museums or art galleries?
4 exciting for a three-day holiday?
5 traffic jams?
6 expensive to live in?
7 efficient public transport system?
8 crowded?
9 .... ?
10 .... ?

❺ Write the first paragraph of a travel article comparing two or three places you know.

Hotel file. Recording vocabulary with pictures

1 Which hotel facilities are the most important for you

a. on a business trip?   b. on a family holiday?

2 Match the symbols below with the list of hotel facilities.

7 2 1 8 5 4 10 9 6 3

1 RESTAURANT	**6** CONFERENCES AND MEETINGS
2 COCKTAIL BAR	**7** IN-ROOM HAIR-DRYERS
3 AIR-CONDITIONING	**8** FITNESS CENTRE
4 SWIMMING-POOL	**9** IN-ROOM SAFES
5 FACILITIES FOR DISABLED	**10** TENNIS COURTS

3 Role-play. Work in pairs.

Student A   You are organizing a conference at the Glenview Hotel. Look at your notes. Phone the Conference Manager and ask about facilities and prices.

Student B   You are the Conference Manager for Glenview Hotel. Look at the information and answer Student A's questions.

Example   **Student A** *Do you have a swimming-pool?*
             Student B *Yes, and a sauna.*

Student A

Meeting 9–10 May (Conference visitors)

Names and special requests
Ms Bailey (likes to swim – swimming-pool?)
Dr Richards (likes to stay fit – sports facilities?)
Mr and Mrs Crocket (Mr C in a wheelchair – facilities for disabled people?)
Mr and Mrs Ramsey (like opera – near Opera House?)

General
• Six people arriving in two cars (parking?)
• Need two double rooms and two single rooms with balconies for night of 9th (prices?)
• All want lunch together on 10th in hotel (restaurant in hotel?)

Student B

★★★★   **Glenview Hotel**   67 rooms
AND CONVENTION CENTRE
— SYDNEY —

Hotel rooms	Standard	Deluxe	Balcony
Single room	A$125	A$145	A$165
Double or twin-bedded room	A$ 145	A$170	A$200

Prices include continental breakfast and service charge.
Opera House, Rocks, and Darling Harbour 5 min by car.
Free car parking for 50 cars. Meeting rooms 5–250 people.

4 Look at the picture of the hotel bathroom and write the correct numbers in the key.

Key	
8	bath
10	shower
11	tap
1	toilet
4	shaver socket
6	hair-dryer
9	towel
3	bathrobe
5	soap
7	toothbrush
2	toothpaste

The eighth wonder of the world

1 Read the company notice and answer the question. Who is the holiday for?

Premier Real Estate

STAFF NEWS

This year it's Australia's Great Barrier Reef!

As usual we are offering our most successful sales staff an exotic holiday to the 'eighth wonder of the world' as a reward for their performance.
This year's destination is Australia's Great Barrier Reef.

4.4 **2** The company asked a travel consultant to present a choice of three islands. Listen to the consultant's presentation and complete the table.

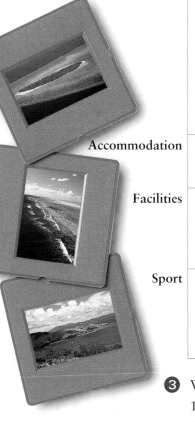

	Hamilton	Heron	Bedarra
General information	largest island, widest choice of activities		smaller, more exclusive than other two
Accommodation		lower prices	
Facilities			
Sport		scuba-diving, snorkelling	

3 Work in groups. The company selected the following sales people for the holiday.

1 Three middle managers, aged 30–45.

2 Three senior managers, aged 40–50.

3 Nine sales representatives, aged 25–35.

Choose the most suitable island for each set of people. Present your choice to the other groups. Give reasons for your choice.

4 Project. Select some of your colleagues to send on a holiday, or choose one of the groups of people from 3 above. Prepare a brief presentation, comparing two or three holiday places you know. Give reasons for recommending the places for a holiday. Give the presentation to your class.

4.5 **1**   Read the faxes. Then listen to the phone call James makes to the hotel. Answer the questions below.

```
12:56     INTERNATIONAL MAGAZINES------- NO.259      P001
```

Wine & Dine
International Magazines Inc

im 15 Honeywell Street London EC4 1DT
Tel: 0171 331 8579
Fax: 0171 331 2280

To   Hotel Leon d'Oro, Verona
From   James Turner
Date   20 March

I am attending Vinitaly in Verona and would like to reserve a single room for four nights, from 3 to 6 April. Please send confirmation of this booking by fax.

James Turner

```
16:56     HOTEL LEON D'ORO, VERONA------- NO.704      P001
```

HOTEL LEON D'ORO
34, Piazza Rasso, 80057, Verona – ITALY
Tel:045-596378 Fax: 045-597878

To   *Mr J Turner*   **From**   *Hotel Leon d'Oro, Verona*
Date   *21 March*

Thank you for your fax. We have reserved a single room for you for four nights from 3 to 6 April.
We look forward to welcoming you on 3 April.

1   What does James want to do?

2   What is the problem?

4.5 **2**   Listen again and complete this part of the conversation.

R   Oh, yes, Mr Turner. I remember.

J   I'd like to book a ...., for a colleague, for 4 April.

R   Let me see. Oh, ..., Mr Turner, but we're fully booked on 4 April, because of Vinitaly, you see.

J   Oh, ...

R   You could try the other hotels in Verona.

J   Yes, I'll do that. .... Goodbye.

4.6 **3**   James checks in at the hotel. Listen to his conversation with the receptionist and tick (✓) the phrases you hear.

I'd like a room, please.
I have a reservation.
Could you fill in this form, please, and sign here?
Here's your key.
Here's your keycard.
Have you got a suitcase?
The porter will take your luggage.
Could I have an early morning call, at 6.30?
Do you need anything else?

4.7 **4**   James checks out of the hotel. Listen to the conversation and tick (✓) T (true) or F (false).

           T   F

1   The hotel doesn't accept credit cards.

2   James wants to stay at the hotel again.

4.7 🔊 **5** Listen again and complete this part of the conversation.

J .... my bill, please? .... by credit card or eurocheque?

R Yes, ... both.

J I'll pay ...., then.

R That's fine. I hope .... your stay here.

J Oh, yes, ...

6 Work in pairs. Role-play these situations.

Student A You are a wine importer and want to go to Vinitaly.	**Student B** You are a receptionist at the hotel.
Situation 1 Telephone the Hotel Due Torri in Verona to book a single room for 4 and 5 April.	**Situation 1** Answer the telephone. Accept the booking.
Situation 2 You want to bring two colleagues with you so you need two more rooms. Telephone the hotel again and try to change the booking.	**Situation 2** Answer the telephone again. One guest cancelled this morning. You have one room available on 4 and 5 April.

Student A You are now the receptionist at the hotel.	**Student B** You are now a guest at the hotel.
Situation 3 Welcome your guest. Check the reservation is for a single room for two nights. Ask the guest to complete and sign the registration form. The guest's room is number 43 on the second floor.	**Situation 3** Arrive and check in at the Hotel Due Torri in Verona. Ask for an early morning call. Ask about breakfast.
Situation 4 Check out your guest. The hotel accepts credit cards. Wish your guest a good trip back.	**Situation 4** Check out of the hotel. Ask if you can pay by credit card.

REVIEW
UNIT A

This unit reviews all the main language points from units 1–4. Complete the exercises. Check your learning with the Self-check box at the end.

❶ Present Simple and frequency adverbs

Interview a partner about work habits. Tick your partner's answers in the questionnaire below.

Example   **Student A** *How often do you arrive at work before your colleagues?*
                Student B *Usually.*

ARE YOU A WORKAHOLIC?

How often do you...	usually	often	sometimes	rarely	never
1 arrive at work before your colleagues?					
2 leave work after normal hours?					
3 take work home at weekends?					
4 think about work when you are at home?					
5 make tiring business trips?					
6 continue working when you are very tired?					

Now add up the score and tell your partner the results:
usually=5 often=4 sometimes=3 rarely=2 never=1

24–30   Be careful! You are becoming a workaholic!
16–23   Try to relax a little more.
 9–15   You are well organized.
 6–8   You are very relaxed!

❷ Frequency adverbs

Make true sentences about your lifestyle. Add five more sentences. Use the frequency adverbs in the box.

Example   *I sometimes go out to restaurants in the evening.*

always
usually
often
sometimes
rarely
never

1 watch the news on TV
2 meet friends at weekends
3 go jogging
4 get up before 7 a.m.
5 read a newspaper
6 study English
7 take work home
8 go to bed after midnight
9 drive to work

❸ Present Simple questions and short answers

Work in pairs. Match A and B below. Then prepare questions in the Present Simple to ask your partner. Use short answers.

A
speak
play
write
make
give
work
read
attend

B
letters in English
meetings or conferences
business trips
English on the phone
a sport
professional literature
presentations
flexitime

Example   **Student A** *Do you speak English on the phone at work?*
                Student B *Yes, I do.*

4 **Present Simple, Present Continuous, or Past Simple?**

Complete the text with the correct form of the verb in brackets.

TRAVEL WRITER ON SAFARI

Jan Allen is a travel writer. She _writes_ [1](write) travel articles for international magazines. Last year she _moved_ [2](move) to Montreal, Canada, where she _lived_ [3](live) with her husband and teenage son, but she _wasn't_ [4](not be) at home very often because she _spent_ [5](spend) more than 50% of her time travelling! At present, she _does_ [6](do) research for an article on safari holidays in Africa. She _visits_ [7](visit) organizations which _specialize_ [8](specialize) in adventure holidays, and she _interviews_ [9](interview) people who _have_ [10](have) experience of safari holidays.

Two months ago, she _flew_ [11](fly) to Africa and _spent_ [12](spend) five weeks travelling around Kenya.

When she _was_ [13](be) there, she _joined_ [14](join) a group of people on a safari holiday and _talked_ [15](talk) to them about the experience.

She _enjoyed_ [16](enjoy) the African trip but she _didn't like_ [17](not like) the mosquitoes! Jan really _loved_ [18](love) travelling because she _met_ [19](meet) all kinds of people. What _does_ she _enjoy_ [20](enjoy) after months of travelling? She usually _likes_ [21](like) to spend a few days at home after a trip, doing absolutely nothing at all.

5 **Past Simple questions**

You asked a friend about her holiday. She gave you these answers. What were your questions?

Example   With Iberia.
           Which airline did you fly with?

1 To Majorca.
2 Only for five days.
3 No, it wasn't. I first went there two years ago.
4 At a hotel on the beach.

5 Yes, it was delicious. And the wines were very good, too.
6 I did a lot of sunbathing and swimming.
7 It was very good. Sunny and hot every day.
8 Yes, I did. I lost my passport!

6 **Comparative and superlative adjectives: quick test**

What are the comparative and superlative forms of these adjectives? Add more examples.

1 few	fewer	fewest
2 lively	liv	
3 crowded		
4 good	better	best
5 suitable		
6 much/many		

7 far		
8 bad	worse	worst
9 enjoyable		
10 little	less	least
11 big	biger	bigest
12 easy	easier	easiest

7 Introductions and greetings

Work in pairs. Give a suitable response to these introductions and greetings.

1 How do you do.
2 Pleased to meet you.
3 Please call me John.
4 How's the family?
5 How are you?
6 How's life?
7 It was very nice meeting you.
8 Have a good trip back.

8 Welcoming a visitor

Look at the photograph. You are welcoming these visitors from another country. Think of five questions to ask the visitors. Ask about their journey, the reason for their visit, their job, their home town, and their first impressions.

9 Telephoning: making contact

Complete this telephone conversation.

A Good morning. *Wine and Dine* magazine.

B Good morning. ....¹Duncan Ross, please?

A Who ....², please?

B ....³ James Turner.

A Hold ....⁴ please, Mr Turner. I'm sorry.

  Mr Ross ....⁵. Can I ....⁶?

B Yes. ....⁷ to call me? My number is 0171 986 5053.

A Yes. Mr Turner. ....⁸.

B Thank you. Goodbye.

⑩ Telephoning: leaving messages

Work in pairs. Practise these telephone calls. Make up two more calls. Change roles.

Student A

Student B

Situation 1

Phone Ian Bell. Your number is 56767.

Situation 1

Ian Bell is in a meeting. Take a message.

Situation 2

Phone the Sales Director of Whole Foods Ltd. Your number is 774884.

Situation 2

You work for Whole Foods Ltd. The Sales Director is on holiday. Take a message.

⑪ Vocabulary

Work in two groups, A and B. Write a vocabulary test to give to the other group. Choose ten of the words below. Write a sentence or phrase to help the other group guess each word.

Example   Word *guest*
           Clue   *A person who stays at a hotel, or who you invite to your house.*

luggage	key	bridge	beach	colleagues
noisy	~~guest~~	shower	suitcase	expensive
daughter	translator	accommodation	job satisfaction	suburbs
salary	currently	appointment	message	delay

⑫ Vocabulary test

Give your vocabulary test to the other group. Return the test for checking.

Look at the self-check box below. Tick the areas you need to review again.

SELF-CHECK BOX	Yes	No	Pocket Book
● Present Simple			2
● Frequency adverbs			2
● Present Continuous			3
● Past Simple			4
● Comparative and superlative adjectives			5
● Introductions and greetings			17
● Welcoming a visitor			18
● Telephoning: making contact			18
● Telephoning: leaving messages			18
● Vocabulary			

UNIT 5
Have a pleasant flight!

Language focus

1 People often feel tired after travelling by plane. What sort of problems do they sometimes have? What can passengers on long flights do to feel better?

2 Look at the description of British Airways' *Well-being in the air* programme. What advice does the programme give passengers about food, drink, and exercise?

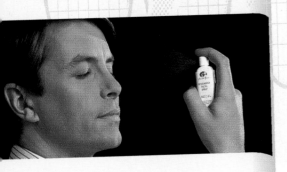

WELL-BEING
IN THE AIR

At British Airways, we know a lot about the problems of frequent flying and jet-lag. That's why we asked our medical experts to create the *Well-being in the air* programme. This programme gives you advice on what to eat and drink in the air, and suggests exercise and relaxation techniques, to help you feel well during and after your flight.

On a long flight, you can feel tired, stiff, and uncomfortable. We invite you to try some of the exercises in the *Well-being* programme. The *Well-being in the air* brochure suggests exercises which help to reduce tiredness and stiffness during and after your flight.

We suggest that you don't drink any alcohol, tea, or coffee during your flight, because they increase the bad effects of flying on the body. It's better to drink a lot of mineral water or fruit juice. We also recommend the dishes on our *Well-being* menu. They are light and easy to digest, and do not have any rich or fatty foods.

Adapted from British Airways'
Well-being in the air brochure.

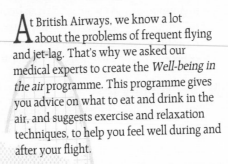

W E L L - B E I N G

5.1 ▢ **3** Listen to a conversation between Ann and a colleague, Martyn. As you listen, tick T (true) or F (false).

	T	F
1 Ann's trip to New York was a holiday.		
2 She did the *Well-being in the air* programme on the flight to New York.		
3 She felt very well after the return flight.		
4 The *Well-being* meals are lighter than the normal menu meals.		
5 The passengers on Ann's flight drank more mineral water than champagne.		

5.1 ▢ **4** Listen to the conversation again and underline the correct alternative.

Example　　*Ann* │ *had a lot of*　　*time to see New York.*
　　　　　　　　│ *didn't have much*

1 When she arrived in New York she │ had some　　problems with jet-lag.
　　　　　　　　　　　　　　　　　│ didn't have any

2 She thinks the *Well-being in the air* programme made │ a lot of　difference.
　　　　　　　　　　　　　　　　　　　　　　　　　　　│ some

3 She │ drank a lot of　alcohol.
　　　│ didn't drink any

4 She didn't eat │ any　　meat.
　　　　　　　　　│ much

5 She did │ some　　exercises on the plane.
　　　　　　│ a lot of

6 │ A lot of　　passengers did the exercises.
　│ Not many

7 The other passengers │ didn't drink much　champagne.
　　　　　　　　　　　　│ drank a lot of

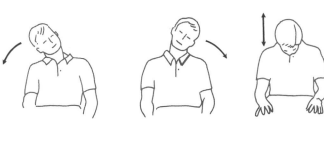

Mass and count nouns

Write the mass and count nouns from the box in the correct columns.
Complete the grammar rules.

magazine	**Mass**	**Count**
coffee	fish	seat
plane	*exercise	*exercises
information	pasta	menu
problem	*time	*times
alcohol	*food	*foods
champagne	alcohol x	mags x
passenger	champagne x	← coffee
fruit juice	fruit juice x	plans x
vegetable	sleep x	← infrmatons x
sleep	vegetable x →	problems x
luggage	luggage x	passengers x
trip	information x	← advice
advice		trip

- Count nouns have a singular and plural form. We can count them.
- Mass nouns do not have a .... form. We cannot count them.
- Some *nouns are both mass and .... count ....

some and any

Read the examples. Complete the grammar rules.

some	**any**
Ann did **some** exercises.	Ann didn't drink **any** alcohol.
Would you like **some** champagne?	She didn't have **any** problems.
Could I have **some** water?	Did she drink **any** coffee?
	Did she have **any** meetings?

- Use *some* in positive sentences, and for offers and requests.
- Use .... in negative sentences, and for questions.
- Use .... and .... with both mass and count nouns.

a lot of/much/many

Read the examples. Complete the grammar rules.

Positive
Ann had **a lot of** meetings in New York.
The *Well-being* programme made **a lot of** difference.

Negative
Ann didn't have **much** time to see New York.
She didn't do **many** exercises on the plane.

Questions
How **much** champagne did they drink?
Did **many** passengers do the exercises?

- Use *a lot of* with both mass and .... nouns in positive sentences.
- Use *much* with mass nouns in negative sentences and in ....
- Use .... with count nouns in .... sentences and in questions.

 Pocket Book p. 6

Practice **1** Complete the sentences with *some* or *any*.

Example   Are there *any* window seats left?

1 I'd like ....*some*............ information about flights to Madrid.

2 Have you got ....*any*............ hand luggage?

3 I'd like to change ....*some*............ travellers' cheques, please.

4 I'm afraid there aren't ....*any*............ seats left in business class.

5 Would you like ....*some*............ magazines?

6 Could I have ....*some*............ more champagne?

7 I didn't buy ....*any*............ duty-free whisky.

8 Would you like ....*some*............ more coffee?

9 Did you buy ....*any*............ duty-free goods?

10 I bought ....*some*............ cigarettes.

2 Ann wrote a letter to a friend she visited during her business trip.
Complete the sentences with *a lot of*, *much*, or *many*.

Dear Jane

It was good to see you in New York last week. Unfortunately I had ......*a lot of*......[1] meetings every

day, so I didn't have ......*much*......[2] free time. I didn't visit ......*many*......[3] of the interesting

places you recommended. I made ......*a lot of*......[4] useful contacts and, with luck, we can do

......*a lot of*......[5] business in the States next year. I know you don't have ......*many*......[6] free

days on your visits, but please try to come and see us. There are ......*many*......[7] interesting

places in London, too. I'm sure you don't know ......*many*......[8] of them!

Love

    Ann

Pronunciation   **①** Listen to these words. What is the sound in the underlined syllables?

5.2   alc*o*hol   inf*or*mation   lem*o*n   The sound is /ə/.

5.3 **②** Listen to the words on the tape. Mark the syllable where you hear the main stress.

Example   po*ta*to   1 magazine   3 exercise   5 problem   7 vegetable
                         2 passenger   4 advice   6 cigarette   8 brochure

5.3 **③** Listen again. Underline where you hear the sound /ə/.

④ Repeat the words. Practise the pronunciation.

---

3 Work in pairs. How do you spend your time every week? Fill in the table. Prepare
questions for a colleague using the table below.

Examples   *How many hours a day do you work?*
             How much time do you spend on sport or exercise?

TIME SURVEY

	Your time 🕐	Your partner's time 🕐
work		
home		
sport		
sleep		
overtime		
watching TV		

4 Interview one person from another pair. Make a note of your partner's answers.

5 Compare the lifestyles of the people in your class.

Food file. Word groups

1 Work in pairs. Look at this menu from Claret's restaurant. Write the different kinds of meat, fish, vegetables, and fruit under the correct headings.

STARTERS

Smoked Scottish salmon

King prawns with herb butter

Duck pâté

Salad of artichoke hearts

—ⓒ—

MAIN COURSE

Grilled trout with almonds served
with a crispy salad

Roast Normandy pork cooked in
a cream and mushroom sauce

Veal cutlets with sautéed potatoes
and onions

Chicken with lemon sauce

Whole Dover sole grilled or fried,
with fresh green beans

—ⓒ—

DESSERTS

Strawberries and cream

Selection of fresh fruit sorbets

Bananas with rum

Yoghurt with figs and passion fruit

Meat

_____

Poultry

duck

_____

Fish/Seafood

salmon

_____

Vegetables

artichokes

_____

Fruit

_____

2 Think of five other foods you know and add them to the lists.

3 Look at the menu again. Underline any methods of cooking.
Example   *Grilled trout with almonds*

4 Which of these methods of cooking do the pictures show? Write *fried*, *grilled*, or *roast*.

....

5 Work in groups. Think of your favourite dish but don't say the name. Find out the favourite dish of each person in your group. Ask questions until you have the correct answer.
Examples   *Is it a main course?*   *How do you cook it?*
Does it contain meat?   *Which other dish is it like?*
What are the ingredients?

6 Work in groups. Prepare a menu for four foreign visitors to your company. The group consists of two Europeans (one is a vegetarian), a Japanese, and an American. Suggest at least one starter, one main course, and one dessert.

Why are the French so lucky?

1 Work in pairs. Answer the questions. Then read the text below to check your answers.

1 Which country in Europe has one of the lowest rates of heart disease?
a. the UK   b. Germany   c. France

2 Why is a daily aspirin good for you?

3 Which meat has more fat, beef or chicken?

4 Which countries do these come from? What do they all have in common?
a. *aioli*   b. *gambas al ajillo*   c. *bruschetta*   d. *tzatziki*

(HEALTH MATTERS)

*Wh*y are the French so lucky?

That was the question medical researchers wanted to answer. The French eat much more cheese than other Europeans but they have the lowest rate of heart disease. Cheese is bad for the heart because, like butter and cream, it has a lot of fat. The results of research are surprising, and good news for wine lovers everywhere. The French are also the biggest wine drinkers in Europe and drinking wine with food reduces the risk of heart attack. And if you're not a wine lover? No problem, a daily aspirin has the same result.

The ancient Greeks were also lucky, it seems. Their diet of olive oil, garlic, fish, vegetables, and bread was very healthy. They ate very little meat, fat, or sugar. The experts today tell us to eat less meat and more vegetables, fruit, fish, pasta, bread, and potatoes. Chicken is healthier than beef because it has less fat. Garlic, the basis of French *aioli*, Spanish *gambas al ajillo*, Italian *bruschetta* and Greek *tzatziki*, also has a good effect on the heart, as well as other benefits, which is perhaps why the ancient Greeks ate so much of it. So, if you love your heart, add a little more garlic and wine to your diet!

Food and Health International magazine

2 Discuss these questions.

1 Do you think your national diet is a healthy diet?

2 Which 'unhealthy' foods do you enjoy eating?

3 When do people in your country usually eat the biggest meal of the day? Do you think it's the best time to eat it?

3 Project. Choose one of the following ideas.

Prepare a short talk about another country's cuisine. Compare it with your national cuisine and say what you like or dislike about it.

Work in groups. Your company wants a new staff restaurant. Discuss your ideas for an interesting, healthy menu and write your suggestions under headings, e.g. Starters, Hot dishes, Cold dishes, Desserts, Snacks, Drinks. Present your ideas to the other groups.

At a restaurant

WHITE WINES
Sancerre
Frascati
Muscadet
Chablis
Chardonnay

RED WINES
Rioja
Chianti
Beaujolais
Burgundy
Corbières
Pinot Noir

5.4 **1** Monique and James are in a restaurant. Listen to their conversation. Tick what they order on the Claret's menu on p. 42 and wine list above.

5.5 **2** Listen to the next part of their conversation. Who do you think pays the bill?

5.6 **3** Listen to the final part of their conversation. Why do you think James asks Monique about her birthday?

5.4, 5.5, 5.6 **4** Listen to the conversations again. Tick the phrases you hear.

Recommending
What do you recommend?
The … is usually excellent here.
I recommend…

Offering
Do have some more…
What about…?
How about…?
Would you like…?

Thanking and responding
Thank you for a really excellent meal.
Thank you for a lovely evening.
Don't mention it.
I enjoyed it very much, too.

Ordering
I'll/We'll have…
I'd/We'd like…
Could we have…?

Accepting
Yes. I'd like that.
Yes. That would be very nice.

Declining
Thank you, but I couldn't eat any more.
No, thank you.

5 Complete the conversation in Claret's restaurant. Use the menu from Claret's and the phrases in 4. Pat is the host and Steve is the guest.

Pat Right. Let's order.

Steve Hmm... It all looks good. What .... ?

Pat Well, for a starter .... , and for the main course .... ?

Steve Yes, ...

Pat And .... to drink?

Steve ....

Pat Yes, ...

(*Later*)

Pat Now, ... a dessert?

Steve Thank you, but ....

Pat .... sure? .... a coffee or a cognac?

Steve ....

(*At the end of the meal*)

Steve Thank you ....

Pat ....

6 Work in pairs. You are in a restaurant.
Student A You are the host/hostess.
Student B You are the guest.

Practise the conversation. Then change roles.

Student A

Ask B what he/she would like.

                Student B

                Ask for a recommendation.

Recommend a starter/main dish.

                Say what you would like.

Offer a drink: wine/beer.

                Say what you would like.

(*Later*)

Offer a dessert/coffee/cognac.

                Reply. Thank A.

Reply to thanks.

7 Work in groups of three or more. You are in a restaurant. One person is the waiter/waitress, another is the host/hostess and the others are guests. Use the Claret's menu. Ask the waiter/waitress and the host/hostess to recommend and describe dishes on the menu.

UNIT 6
A suitable candidate?

▼ AGENDA

▶ Past Simple and Present Perfect Simple, *ever*

▶ Recruitment file. Word map

▷ How to succeed at an interview

▷ Making arrangements

Language focus **1** Read the job advertisement. Answer the questions.

1 Why are 'excellent interpersonal and presentation skills' important in this job?
2 Would you like this job? Give your reasons.

Business Development Manager

The TransEurope Luxury Train (TELT) is the most exciting new concept of this decade. It provides exclusive facilities for leisure and corporate entertainment as it travels through the most beautiful parts of Europe.

We are looking for a creative, energetic person to market luxury travel packages to the leisure and corporate travel industry worldwide. You must have excellent interpersonal and presentation skills, experience of working in the leisure and/or corporate travel sector, and enjoy international travel and contact. Ideally, you are 27–35 years old, and fluent in English and two other European languages.

Attractive salary, car, and bonus.

Please apply to:

Euro-Executive Search,

Box No 1329, rue de la Loi 187, 1049 Brussels

2 Read the curriculum vitae from one of the applicants for this job, and extracts from his letter. Match the letter extracts to the relevant parts of his CV.

...As you can see from my CV, I studied hotel management and tourism in Switzerland for three years... (1)

...After I obtained my diploma in 1987, I worked in France for two years and became fluent in French. This position gave me experience of the leisure sector of the hotel industry... (2)

...As manager, I was responsible for the planning and organization of large conferences ... (3)

...In my present job I have travelled a lot in Europe, and have made many important contacts in the corporate travel sector...

...Recently I have been responsible for making promotional videos for our marketing programmes...

...The results of my marketing programmes have been excellent. Corporate business in all the Group's hotels has increased significantly... (4)

Curriculum vitae

Personal details
NAME:	Erwin Verhoot
DATE OF BIRTH:	2.10.66
NATIONALITY:	Dutch
ADDRESS:	Van Baerlestraat 54, 1070 Amsterdam
TEL. NO:	020 6725331

Qualifications
1987   Diploma in Hotel Management and Tourism. Swiss Hotel Management School, Montreux

Professional experience

1993-Present   Corporate Client Services Manager
Palace Hotels Group, Brussels.
Responsible for marketing corporate client services of Group's five 4-star European hotels.

1990-1993   Manager
Capital Hotel, Amsterdam. 180 room, 4-star hotel with over 70% business clients. Conference facilities for 100 people.

1987-1989   Assistant Manager
Hotel Mont Blanc, Chamonix. 150 room, 3-star hotel.

Languages   Dutch, English, German, French.

3 Underline the verbs in the letter extracts. Which tense does Erwin Verhoot use to describe his previous jobs? Does he use the same tense to talk about his current job?

Past Simple and Present Perfect Simple

Read the examples. Complete the grammar rules.

Past Simple

- I **obtained** my Diploma in 1987.
- I **worked** in France for two years.

Present Perfect Simple

- In my present job I **have travelled** a lot in Europe.
- The results **have been** excellent.
- Corporate business **has increased** significantly.

- To make the Present Perfect Simple, use .... or ....
  + the past participle of the verb (*travelled*, *been*, *increased*).

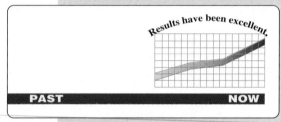

- Use the .... for finished situations and actions in the past.

- Use the Present Perfect Simple for past actions and situations in a period up to the present.

- Use the .... for past actions with present results.

Pocket Book p. 7

6.1 ▢ **4** Read the CV from another applicant, Olivia Lonro. Listen to part of her interview. Make a note of her answers in the notebook opposite.

CURRICULUM VITAE

Personal Details

Name:	Olivia Lonro	Date of Birth:	8.8.68
Address:	23 Condale Ave,	Tel. No:	0171 491 7320
	London SW1 2DX	Nationality:	British

Qualifications

1989   BA Hons. Business degree. European Business School, London.

Professional Experience

1994–Present   Marketing Director, Worldwide Cruises, London. Responsible for marketing activities in leisure and corporate entertainment sectors.

1990–1994   Marketing Consultant, Hotel Marketing Concepts, London. Responsible for marketing quality leisure hotels.

Languages   English, French, German, Japanese.

INTERVIEW NOTES

Name: Olivia Lonro   11.30 a.m.   4 March

- (First job with Hotel Marketing Concepts)
  1 Which markets was she responsible for?...

  ....

- (Speaks Japanese!)
  2 Has she ever been to Japan?..

  ....

- (Knowledge of Japanese market important for this job)
  3 Has she had any contact with Japan in her present job?................................

  ....

- (Experience of train travel, e.g. Orient Express)
  4 Has she ever travelled on a luxury train?..

  ....

Present Perfect Simple questions, *ever*

Read the examples of Present Perfect Simple questions. Answer the questions.

- **Has** she **had** any contact with Japan?   Yes, she **has**.
- **Have** you **ever been** to Japan?   Yes, I **have**.
- **Has** she **ever travelled** on a luxury train?   No, she **hasn't**.

Have you ever ✈ been to Japan ?

PAST   NOW

1 How do we make Present Perfect Simple questions?
2 What is the difference between *She's gone to Japan* and *She's been to Japan*?
3 Which word do we use for 'at any time in your life' in Present Perfect questions?

 Pocket Book p. 7

Practice **1** Quick test. Complete the table.

Infinitive	Past Simple	Past Participle
buy	*bought*	*bought*
do		
eat		
give		
go		
make		
meet		
read		
see		
write		

Check your answers in the Pocket Book p. 16.

2 Work in pairs. Ask and answer five questions and add two more. Tick the things your partner has done.

Example **Student A** *Have you had a holiday this year?*
Student B *No, I haven't.*

Student A	Student B	Student B	Student A
1 have/a holiday this year?	....	1 eat/any foreign food recently?	....
2 buy/anything expensive recently?	....	2 write/any letters this week?	....
3 make/any business trips in the last three months?	....	3 have/a birthday in the last six months?	....
4 do/any sport this week?	....	4 see/any good films this month?	....
5 meet/any foreigners this month?	....	5 read/any good books recently?	....
6	....	6	....
7	....	7	....

3 Complete this extract from the interviewer's report on Olivia Lonro. Use the Simple Past or Present Perfect Simple tense.

INTERVIEW NOTES

Name: Olivia Lonro 11.30 a.m.   4 March

In her career, Ms Lonro has travelled [1](travel) widely in Europe, the USA, and the Far East. She (has) made [2](make) many useful contacts in the countries she (has) visited [3](visit). In 1993, she spent [4](spend) one month in Japan and met [5](meet) the key people in the tourist industry there. Her professional experience has given [6](give) her a wide knowledge of the luxury holiday market. This year she has produced [7](produce) a promotional video for the US market. She has never travelled [8](never, travel) on a luxury train, but she travelled [9](travel) across China by train when she was [10](be) a student.

6.2

① Listen to the examples. Notice how *have* and *has* sound different in a. and b.

a. I don't think I have.   b. Have you heard this before?
a. He hasn't arrived.   b. Robert has forgotten.

6.3 ② Listen to these sentences. Which sound do you hear? Write a. or b.

1 .... 2 .... 3 .... 4 .... 5 .... 6 .... 7 .... 8 ....

③ Write down as many questions as you can in two minutes. All questions should begin *Have you...*

④ Work in pairs. Ask and answer each other's questions.

④ Work in pairs. You and your partner have both applied for the job at TELT. Interview your partner. Ask and answer the questions below. Add two more questions. If the answer is 'Yes, I have', ask for more details.

Example   **Student A** *Have you ever worked in the hotel business?*
Student B *Yes, I have.*
Student A *When was that? Where did you work?*

		Yes/No	Details
1	work/in the tourist industry?	☐	....
2	do/any marketing or sales?	☐	....
3	give/any presentations?	☐	....
4	study/any European languages?	☐	....
5	travel/on a luxury train?	☐	....
6	go/on a cruise?	☐	....
7	organize/a conference or other corporate activity?	☐	....
8	want/to work in the luxury travel industry?	☐	....
9	....	☐	....
10	....	☐	....

⑤ Is your partner a suitable candidate for the job? Give reasons for your opinion.
Example   *He/She is a suitable candidate because he/she has done a lot of marketing.*

⑥ Work in groups. Erwin Verhoot and Olivia Lonro are the top candidates for the job of Business Development Manager. Look at the TELT job advertisement again. Compare the qualifications and work experience of the two candidates. Decide who is the more suitable person for the job. Give your reasons.

⑦ Write a memo to the Personnel Director of the parent company, *Travel Enterprises*, stating which candidate you have chosen. Give reasons for your choice.

Recruitment file. Word map

1 Work in pairs. Complete the word map with the words from the box.
Use your dictionary to check new words.

candidate   experience   interview   job title   personal details   qualifications   salary   working conditions

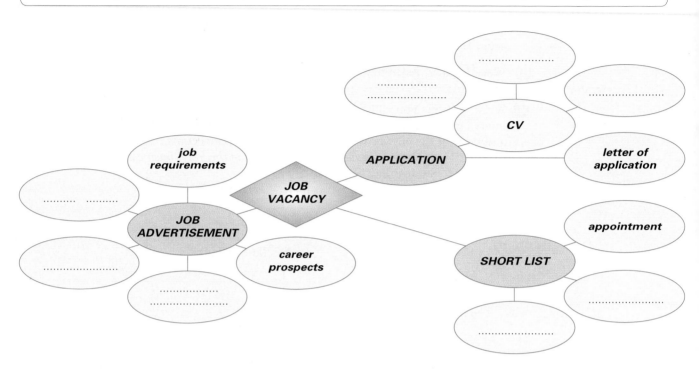

2 Use the words from the word map above to complete this description.

How a company fills a job vacancy

The company usually advertises the j................ v................ ¹ in a newspaper.
The a................ ² usually gives the j................ t................ ³ and a
description of the j................ r................ ⁴. It sometimes gives the
s................ ⁵ and describes the w................ c................ ⁶ and
c................ p................ ⁷ as well.

The applicant usually sends in a letter of a................ ⁸ and a c................
v................ ⁹ or CV, which gives p................ d................ ¹⁰ and lists
qualifications and e................ ¹¹. The company then makes a s................
l................ ¹² of the most suitable candidates and invites them for an
i................ ¹³. The company then chooses the best c................ ¹⁴ and makes
an a................ ¹⁵.

3 Complete the table.

Verb	Activity	Person 1	Person 2
employ	....	....	employee
....	interview	interviewer	....
....	training	....	....

4 Work in groups. Compare how companies usually fill job vacancies in your countries.

5 Work in pairs. Ask questions to find out how your partner got his/her first or present job.

How to succeed at an interview

1 Work in groups. Discuss your answers to this question.
What are the most important things to remember when you attend a job interview?

6.4 **2** Listen to a careers officer giving advice about job interviews. As you listen, complete the list of ten guidelines on preparing for, and attending, an interview.

HOW TO SUCCEED AT AN INTERVIEW

A Preparing for the interview

1 Find out about the company.

2 ....

3 ....

B Attending the interview

4 Dress smartly.

5 ....

6 ....

7 Try to stay positive and relaxed.

8 ....

9 ....

10 ....

3 Work in groups. Look at the list of ten guidelines. Answer the questions.

1 In your opinion, which guidelines are the most important?
2 Can you think of any other advice to give a candidate?

4 Work in groups. Prepare a list of ten guidelines on how to be a good interviewer.

5 Write your CV. Use Erwin Verhoot's CV on p. 47 as a model. What other information can you add to complete yours?

CURRICULUM VITAE

Personal Details

Name: ....   Tel. No: ....

Address: ....   Nationality: ....

....

Qualifications ....

....

Professional Experience ....

....

....

....

....

....

....

....

Languages ....

Hobbies ....

6 Project. Work in groups. Your organization needs a new employee. Decide what kind of person you want. Think about the personal qualities, qualifications, and experience the person needs. Prepare a list of questions to ask at the interview.

Making arrangements

1 Read the letter and answer the question.
Why is Duncan Ross writing to Monique Bresson?

Wine & Dine

International Magazines Inc

15 Honeywell Street London EC4 1DT
Tel: 0171 331 8579
Fax: 0171 331 2280

Ms M Bresson
46, Chapel Street
London
SW1 8QW

Tuesday 1 June

Dear Ms Bresson

I hope you remember me from last year. James Turner introduced us at
Vinexpo, and you gave me your business card. I am writing to you because I
want to publish a French edition of *Wine and Dine* Magazine. I would like to
form a long-term business relationship with a translation agency.

Do you have time to join me for lunch one day, to discuss the possibility of
doing business together? I will telephone you next week and, if you are
interested, we can arrange a meeting.

Yours sincerely

D. Ross

Duncan Ross
Editor and publisher

6.5 **2** Duncan Ross calls Monique a week later. Listen to their conversation and
write down the appointment (day, time, name of restaurant) in Monique's diary.

6.5 **3** Listen to the conversation again and tick the
phrases you hear.

Making an appointment
When would be convenient for you?
When are you free?
Shall we say…
What time would suit you?
Is … possible for you?
How about…?
What about…?

Saying 'yes'
Yes, … suits me fine.
Yes, that's fine.
Yes. I can make it on…
I look forward to meeting you…
See you on…

Saying 'no'
No, I'm afraid I'm busy then.
No, I'm afraid I've got another appointment…

Changing an appointment
I'm very sorry.
I have to cancel the appointment on…
I'm afraid I can't manage our meeting on…
Could we arrange another time?

JUNE

14 Monday   *10.30 Meeting-Anne Camp,*
Elco plc
Lunch John Elliot
P.M. Work on new brochure
6.30 Tennis

15 Tuesday

16 Wednesday
11.00 Italian Trade Centre,
London
7.30 National Theatre-
meet Sue in bar

17 Thursday
a.m. Meeting re. Elco project

18 Friday

4 Monique phones Duncan Ross a few days later. Listen to their conversation and answer the questions.

  1 What is Monique's problem?
  2 Is Duncan free on Thursday 17th?
  3 Which day suits both of them?

5 Listen to their conversation again and tick the phrases you hear in 3 above.

6 Complete the conversation. Use phrases from 3 above to help you.

Andrew	Hello. Is that .... ?
Chris	Yes, speaking.
Andrew	This is .... Could we arrange a meeting to discuss our trip to the UK?
Chris	Of course. .... for you?
Andrew	.... next Tuesday morning?
Chris	No, ... then. .... on Wednesday afternoon?
Andrew	Yes, ...
Chris	.... 2.30?
Andrew	.... See you on Wednesday, then. Goodbye.

7 Work in pairs. Practise making an appointment. Change roles and make an appointment for another meeting.

8 Complete the conversation. Use phrases from 3 above.

Armand	Hello. Is that .... ?
Jan	Yes, ...
Armand	This is .... I'm very sorry. .... Could we .... ?
Jan	Yes, ... When .... ?
Armand	Is .... for you?
Jan	No, ... How about .... ?
Armand	Yes, ...
Jan	Good. ....

9 Work in pairs. Change the appointments you made in 7 above.

10 Work in pairs. Role-play two more phone calls. Telephone your colleague and make an appointment for next week. Ring again and change the appointment.

UNIT 7
Working in another country

▼ AGENDA

▶ Present Perfect Simple and Continuous, *since* and *for*

▶ Trends file. The language of graphs

▷ The Italian fashion industry

▷ Opinions and suggestions. Agreeing and disagreeing

Language focus **1** What do you think of the design of the items in the pictures?

7.1 **2** Susan Hill is a fashion designer who lives and works in Italy. Listen to a radio interview with her and complete the information below.

Name	*Susan Hill*
Nationality	....
City	....
Profession	....
First job in Italy	....
Current work	....
Reason for working abroad	....

3 Read the final part of the interview with Susan Hill. Underline the verb forms. Which tenses are they?

Presenter Have you been to England this year?

Susan No. I haven't had time. I've been travelling a lot recently. I've just visited a factory in Modena, for example, and I've been to Germany a few times since Christmas.

Presenter And have you had any free time in your busy work schedule?

Susan Well, unfortunately, I've had very little free time this year, but I've been visiting friends more in the last few months. I feel that I've been working too much this year, so I've been trying to relax more...

Presenter Well, thank you for talking to us, Susan.

Susan It was a pleasure.

Present Perfect Simple and Present Perfect Continuous

Read the examples. Complete the grammar rules.

Present Perfect Simple

- I've **been** a freelance designer since 1988.
- I've **designed** a lot of fashion items for Italian companies.

- Use the Present Perfect Simple for a situation which began in the past and continues to the present.
- Use the .... for past actions in a time period up to the present when we give the quantity.

Present Perfect Continuous

- How long **have** you **been living** in Florence?
- In the last four years, I've **been designing** for Burberrys.

- To make the Present Perfect Continuous, use *has/have* + ...+ *-ing* form of the verb.
- Use the .... for an action that began in the past and continues to the present.

Do we use the Present Perfect Simple or Continuous to focus on an activity?

Pocket Book p. 8

Practice ① Underline the correct verb form.

1 Susan is working/has been working as a designer since 1982.
2 She has made/has been making three business trips to Milan this month.
3 In the past year, she designs/has been designing handbags for Italian companies.
4 She has travelled/has been travelling to the UK many times since 1988.
5 She has made/has been making a lot of contacts in the fashion industry since 1982.

since and *for*

Read the examples. Complete the grammar rule.

- Susan has been living in Florence **since** 1982.
- She has been a designer **for** many years.

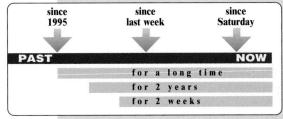

- Use .... with a point in time and .... with a length of time.

② Write *since* or *for* with these time expressions.

1 .... three years   6 .... one o'clock
2 .... a week   7 .... a long time
3 .... yesterday   8 .... my last appointment
4 1990   9 .... ten minutes
5 .... last month   10 .... Monday

3 Complete this fashion magazine article by choosing the Past Simple, Present Perfect Simple, or Present Perfect Continuous form of the verbs in brackets.

*f*ashion fortunes

Since the 1970s, designers like Giorgio Armani, Ralph Lauren, and Calvin Klein *have been* ¹(be) enormously successful. Their companies *have been growing* ²(grow) for more than twenty years and they *have become* ³(become) rich world businessmen. The fashion businesses of French designers like Pierre Cardin and Louis Féraud *have made* ⁴(make) even bigger fortunes. Armani, one of Italy's most successful designers, *started* ⁵(start) his company in 1975 with an investment of $10,000. Since then, his company's turnover *has increased* (increase) steadily, and in recent years it *has grown* ⁷(grow) to $1 billion. ■

4 Work in pairs. Complete the questionnaires from *Which Product?* magazine. Use *since* or *for* in your answers where possible. Add two more products.

Examples *Have you got a…?*   *Yes, I have./No, I haven't.*
          How long have you had it? *I've had it for/since…*
          Have you had any problems with it? *Yes, I have./No, I haven't.*

Student A
Ask Student B questions. Complete the questionnaire.

WHICH PRODUCT? HOME ENTERTAINMENT

		YES/NO	MONTHS/YEARS	PROBLEMS
1	a television set			
2	a video recorder			
3	a cassette player			
4	a personal stereo			
5	a compact disc player			
6	a home computer			
7				
8				

Student B
Ask Student A questions. Complete the questionnaire.

WHICH PRODUCT? ELECTRICAL APPLIANCES

		YES/NO	MONTHS/YEARS	PROBLEMS
1	a washing machine			
2	a dishwasher			
3	an iron			
4	a coffee machine			
5	a microwave oven			
6	a food processor			
7				
8				

① Listen to the conversations. Which listener sounds more interested, a. or b.?

7.2

a. I've lived here for fifteen years.	a. I work in Helsinki.
Have you?	Really?
b. I've lived here for fifteen years.	b. I work in Helsinki.
Have you?	Really?

Mark the intonation patterns. ↗ ↘

7.3 ② Listen to the conversations. Tick the conversations where the listener's voice shows interest.

1 I work in the city centre.
  Do you?

2 I didn't have time to finish yesterday.
  Didn't you?

3 I've been working very hard this week.
  Have you?

4 I don't like jazz.
  Don't you?

5 We went to a restaurant for lunch.
  Did you?

6 I've never visited Rome.
  Haven't you?

7.4 ③ Listen to the conversations. Repeat the listener's words.

❺ Headhunters are people who recruit new staff for companies. Look at the *International Headhunters* profile form below. Prepare questions for a headhunter's general interview. Here are some ideas to help you.

- where they live (how long?)
- where they work (company? job responsibilities? how long?)
- if they travel on business (where? how many trips this year?)
- what languages they're learning (how long?)
- if they have had other jobs (where? when? job responsibilities?)
- what leisure activities they enjoy (how long?)

Examples   *Where do you live?*
           How long have you been living in…?
           Have you travelled much in your present job?

❻ Role-play. Work in pairs.
Student A   You are a headhunter. Interview Student B to complete the Professional profile form.
Student B   You are an interviewee. Answer Student A's questions.

INTERNATIONAL HEADHUNTERS

PROFESSIONAL PROFILE

NAME ....

PRESENT JOB ....
....
....

LENGTH OF TIME ....

RESPONSIBILITIES ....
....
....
....

TRAVEL ....

LANGUAGES ....

PREVIOUS JOBS ....
....
....
....

QUALIFICATIONS ....
....
....

LEISURE INTERESTS ....
....
....

Trends file. The language of graphs

1 Match the verb phrases in the box to the correct graphs.

| to remain stable | to reach a peak | to fall | to level off | to improve |
| to decrease | | to go down | | to go up | to increase |

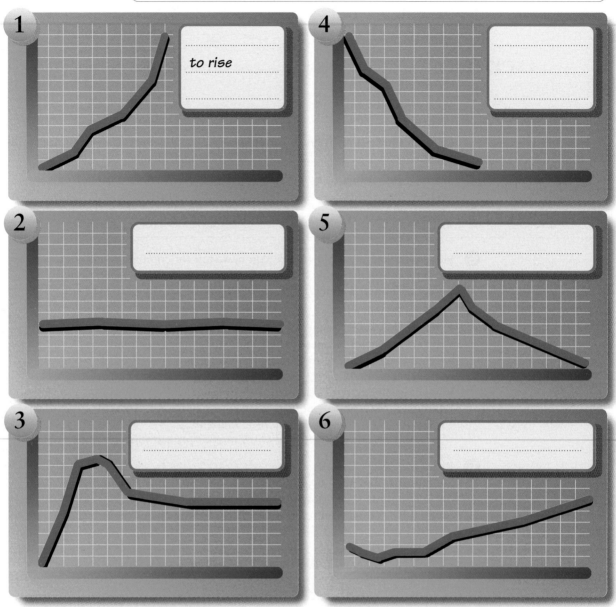

1 *to rise*

4

2

5

3

6

2 Complete the table.

Verb		Noun
Infinitive	Past	
to decrease	....	a ....
....	fell	a ....
....	....	an increase
to rise	....	a ....
....	....	an improvement

3 Match the adjectives/adverbs to the type of change they describe.

adjective/adverb
dramatic/dramatically
sharp/sharply
steady/steadily
slight/slightly

type of change
regular (not sudden)
very small
sudden, large
sudden, very large

4 Read the examples. Complete the sentences with the correct preposition.

Examples

There was a steady rise in sales...

There was a fall of 3% in salaries...

There was an increase of £5...

Inflation remained stable at 2.5%...

Prices rose from $100 to $130...

Salaries rose by 3.5%...

Prices went up by £20...

1 Production costs rose .... 3% last year.

2 Sales remained stable .... an average of 2,000 per month.

3 Inflation went up .... 2.3% .... 2.4% last month.

4 There was a decrease .... 1.5% in unemployment.

5 There was an increase .... prices last year.

5 Look at the graph. Complete the description.

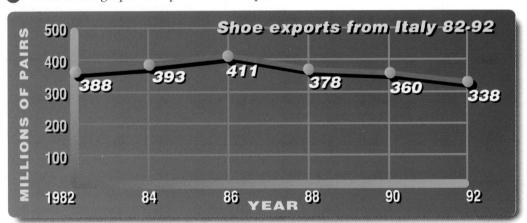

In 1982, Italy exported 388 million pairs of shoes. Exports .... [1] steadily in the next two years, and reached 393 million in 1984. This .... [2] continued and exports .... a .... [3] of 411 million in 1986. In the next two years they fell .... [4] and there was a further .... [5] in 1990, to 360 million. Between 1990 and 1992, they .... [6] again, to 338 million pairs.

6 Look at the graph. Write a description of the trend in shoe imports to Italy from 1982 to 1992.

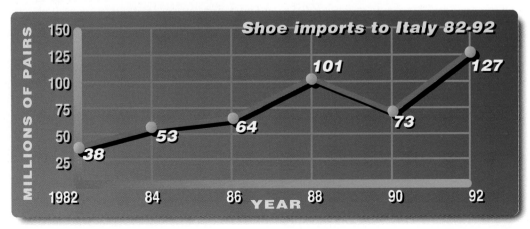

The Italian fashion industry

① Look at these sentences about the Italian fashion industry. Underline the answer you think is correct. Read the text to check your answers.

1 Florence/Milan/Rome is Italy's 'fashion capital'.
2 Italy produces approximately 2/30/400 million pairs of shoes a year.
3 Italy has a trade surplus/deficit in clothing.

11

The Italian fashion industry

Italy's fashion boom began in the 1950s. Since then, fashion – clothing, textiles, and footwear – has become Italy's biggest export industry, worth $30 billion a year. Milan is Italy's 'fashion capital'. It has been the most important centre for 'ready-to-wear' designer fashion since the 1970s. The top Italian designers – Armani, Versace, Valentino, Ferrè – all have their fashion houses there. Every year their new collections attract wide attention. Florence also has several major international fashion events, and Rome is the capital of *l'alta moda* or *haute couture*.

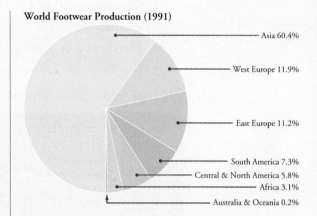

World Footwear Production (1991)

Asia 60.4%
West Europe 11.9%
East Europe 11.2%
South America 7.3%
Central & North America 5.8%
Africa 3.1%
Australia & Oceania 0.2%

Italy is the biggest exporter of clothing and footwear in the European Union. Footwear has a bigger export surplus than clothing, with a revenue six times higher than the value of imports. Exports reached a peak in 1978 when they represented 20% of the total world footwear trade. In 1992, Italy made 419 million pairs of shoes, and exported 338 million pairs. Top of the market are Ferragamo and Gucci. Germany imported 94.5 million pairs of shoes from Italy in 1992, and is Italy's biggest customer for shoes and clothing, followed by France, and then the USA.

The Italian fashion industry is very flexible, and it has remained competitive because it has been able to react quickly to changes in the market. However, in recent years, production costs in Italy have been rising, and imports have been growing faster than exports. Mid-priced clothing in particular has been facing growing competition from countries in the Far East, South America, and Eastern Europe, where labour costs are lower. The export market has remained strong, however. In 1992, the value of exported clothing was $6 billion, more than twice the value of imported clothing.

Italian Footwear Exports 1992
Pairs (000.000)

Germany	94.5
France	48.2
USA	29.7
UK	24.2
CIS	14.6
Netherlands	14.3
Switzerland	14.2
Belgium	13.7
Austria	13.5
Saudi Arabia	5.8
Others	66.0

Source ISTAT data processed by ANCI

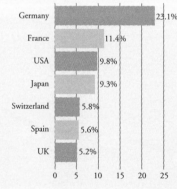

Italian Clothing Exports 1992

Germany	23.1%
France	11.4%
USA	9.8%
Japan	9.3%
Switzerland	5.8%
Spain	5.6%
UK	5.2%

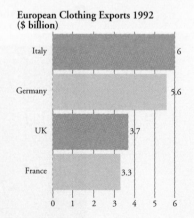

European Clothing Exports 1992
($ billion)

Italy	6
Germany	5.6
UK	3.7
France	3.3

2 Work in pairs. Complete the EuroDatabank on the Italian fashion industry with information from the text and the visuals on p. 62.

EuroDatabank

Italian fashion industry: key figures 1992

A	ITALIAN FASHION EXPORTS

Clothing

Textiles

Footwear

Total value $ billion

B	ITALIAN FOOTWEAR EXPORTS

Principal buyers
Germany
France
USA

Millions of pairs

C	WORLD FOOTWEAR PRODUCTION (1991)

Asia

W Europe

E Europe

Percentage

D	ITALIAN CLOTHING EXPORTS

Principal buyers
....
....
....

Percentage
23.1

E	EUROPEAN CLOTHING EXPORTS

Principal countries
....
....
....
....

Total value $ billion
6
5.6
3.7
3.3

3 Discuss these topics in groups.

1 Which city do you think is Europe's 'fashion capital' today – Milan, Paris, or another? Give your reasons.

2 Fashion has become big business and the top designers have made large fortunes. Why do you think they have been so successful?

3 Which country do you think has the best dressed
   a. women   b. men?

4 Project. Collect some facts and figures about your country, your company, or another organization you are interested in. Prepare a short presentation using graphs and other visuals. Give the presentation to your class.

Opinions and suggestions. Agreeing and disagreeing

7.5 🔊 **1** Listen to the first part of a conversation between Duncan Ross and James Turner. Answer the questions.

1 What celebration does Duncan want to discuss with James?
2 Why does Duncan want to charter a plane?
3 What other event does Duncan suggest they celebrate?
4 What does James think about this idea?

7.5 🔊 **2** Listen again and tick the phrases you hear.

Asking for opinions
What do you think about...?
What's your opinion of...?
How do you feel about...?

Giving opinions
In my opinion...
I think...

Agreeing
I agree.
I certainly agree with that.
I agree completely.

Disagreeing
I'm afraid I don't agree.
I'm sorry, but I disagree.

7.6 🔊 **3** Listen to the second part of their conversation. Tick T (true) or F (false).

	T	F
1 There is a busy programme on the first day.		
2 James thinks the treasure hunt is a good idea.		
3 The last event on the programme is a dinner.		
4 Duncan wants to make sure they've invited everyone.		

7.6 ⏸️ **4** Listen again and tick the phrases you hear.

Making suggestions	**Accepting suggestions**
I suggest...	Yes, that's a good idea.
How about...?	Yes, let's do that.
What about...?	
Why don't we...?	**Rejecting suggestions**
Why not...?	Yes, but...
We could...	I'm not sure about that.
	I'm afraid I don't like that idea.

Asking for suggestions
Do you have any suggestions for...?
Any ideas on...?

5 Match A and B to make suggestions.

A	B
I suggest we	invite some friends for dinner?
How about	spend next Sunday in the country?
What about	going away for a few days?
Why don't we	go to a restaurant in the evening.
Why not	go skiing next weekend.
We could	buying tickets for the music festival?

6 Discuss these statements in groups. Use the phrases in 2 above to ask for and give opinions, and agree or disagree with your colleagues. Add two more topics to this list and discuss them.

1 Flexitime at work is a good idea.
2 Violence on TV is dangerous.

7 Discuss one of these topics in groups. Use the phrases in 4 above to suggest solutions, and accept or reject the ideas of your colleagues.

1 At present your company pays for your English course. Next year, it wants employees to pay 50% of the cost. What can you do to stop this change?

2 It's your company's 50th anniversary next year. Suggest ways of celebrating the occasion.

3 Your town wants to improve its leisure facilities. Suggest changes and improvements.

UNIT 8
A new luxury hotel

▼ AGENDA

▶ Futures: Present Continuous, *going to*

▶ Air travel file. Word map

▷ Flight announcements

▷ Invitations

Language focus ❶ What facilities would you include in a new luxury hotel for international guests?

❷ Look at the brochure of The Pacific Hotel in Jakarta, Indonesia. Would you like to stay in this hotel? Give your reasons.

THE PACIFIC HOTEL

GUEST ROOMS
420 ROOMS
COLOUR TV
CNN
REFRIGERATOR
MINI-BAR
INTERNATIONAL DIRECT DIAL
TELEPHONES
BATHROOMS EN-SUITE
24-HOUR ROOM SERVICE

BUSINESS CENTRE
SECRETARIAL SERVICES
TRANSLATION
TELEX
PHOTOCOPYING
FACSIMILE TRANSMISSION
PERSONAL COMPUTER/
WORD PROCESSING

RESTAURANTS AND BARS
ORIENTAL RESTAURANT
THE PACIFIC GRILL
THE ROOF TOP CAFÉ
THE CLUB BAR

LEISURE FACILITIES
ROOF-TOP GARDEN AND
SWIMMING-POOL
FITNESS ROOM
SAUNA
TENNIS COURTS

3 Read the invitation to the Grand Opening of The Pacific Hotel, and the programme which the hotel manager has sent to journalists. Prepare three questions about the Grand Opening to ask at the Press briefing.

> **Nick Lander** of *Business International*
> is invited to the
>
> ### Grand Opening of The Pacific Hotel, Jakarta
>
> on 20 July and to the
> Press briefing for journalists on 19 July at 19.00
>
> *R S V P*

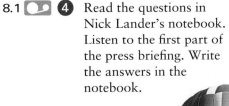

PROGRAMME

10.00	Arrival of President of The Pacific Hotels Group
10.30	Opening speech
11.00	Champagne reception
11.30	Tour of Business Centre
12.30	Buffet lunch: Roof Garden
14.00	Oriental menu presentation
15.00	Tour of hotel rooms and leisure facilities
16.30	Balloon flights
20.00	Dinner: Oriental Restaurant
22.00	Musical extravaganza with fireworks

8.1 **4** Read the questions in Nick Lander's notebook. Listen to the first part of the press briefing. Write the answers in the notebook.

The Pacific Hotel, Jakarta Opening
Questions for press briefing (7 p.m. 19 July)
1 Is the President arriving by car?

2 Where's he making the opening speech?

3 Where's the champagne reception taking place?

4 Is the President taking a balloon flight?

8.2 **5** Listen to Nick Lander and another journalist, Kiki Johns, talking about their plans for the Grand Opening. Complete the sentences.

1 Kiki is going to take a balloon ....

2 Nick is going to take photos of ....

3 Nick is going to write about the hotel's ....

4 The readers of his magazine are all ....

5 Kiki is going to write about the leisure facilities, the .... ,

   and the ....

Futures: Present Continuous, *going to*

Read the examples. Complete the grammar rules.

Present Continuous

- The President **is arriving** by helicopter at 10 a.m.
- We**'re not having** the champagne reception there.
- **Is** the President **taking** a balloon flight in the afternoon?
- Where **is** he **making** the opening speech?

going to

- I**'m going to take** some photos of the President's arrival.
- I**'m not going to describe** the hotel's business facilities.
- **Are** you **going to take** a balloon flight?
- What **are** you **going to write** about?

- Use the .... for fixed future arrangements.

- Use .... for future plans, intentions, and decisions.

Do we normally use *going to* with the verbs *to come* and *to go*?

 Pocket Book p. 9

Practice **1** Nick Lander decided to stay in Jakarta for a few days after the Grand Opening. Look at the arrangements in his diary. Complete the fax he sent to his secretary. Use the verbs in the box.

arrive	have	interview	spend	travel

Example   *I'm staying in Jakarta until the 23rd.*

Mon 19	19.00	Press Briefing – The Pacific Hotel
Tue 20	10.00	Opening PH – all day
Wed 21	13.30	lunch with head of Chamber of Commerce
	16.00	interview Minister of Trade
	16.45	sightseeing tour of city
Thu 22	10.30	visit Juho Rubber Plantation – all day
	20.00	dinner – Kiki Johns (meet bar, Hotel Bali)
Fri 23	11.15	meet exporters at Trade Centre
	18.00	check-in – flight leaves 19.20
Sat 24	05.20	arrive London Heathrow Airport

PACIFIC HOTEL

To   Sue Lowe
From   Nick Lander
Date   20 July

I've changed my plans. Please cancel all appointments in London from 22 to 24 July. I .... [1] back in England on Saturday. I .... [2] on the 19.20 flight from Jakarta on 23 July, landing Heathrow 05.20 on 24 July. I've made some useful contacts. Tomorrow I .... [3] lunch with the head of the Chamber of Commerce and then I .... [4] the Minister of Trade. On 22 July I .... [5] the day on a rubber plantation.

See you on Monday.

Nick

2 Describe Nick Lander's arrangements for 21, 22, and 23 July.

3 Write your arrangements for next week in the diary below. Include two meetings, a short trip, three lunches or dinners, showing a visitor around, and two other arrangements.

Monday	
Tuesday	
Wednesday	
Thursday	
Friday	

4 Work in groups. Arrange the following appointments for times when you are all free. Explain what you are doing when you're not free.

1 a one-hour meeting   3 a two-hour meeting
2 a working lunch   4 a dinner one evening

Example   **Student A** *Is Tuesday morning possible for you?*
                Student B *No, it isn't, I'm afraid. I'm attending a meeting then.*

Pocket Book p. 9

5 Think of three New Year resolutions for next year like the ones below. Explain the reasons for them.

I'm going to spend more time with my family.

I'm going to give up smoking.

I'm going to travel around the world.

I'm going to change my whole life!

Example   *I'm going to do more exercise because I want to be really fit.*

Pronunciation

1 Listen to the two questions on the tape. Notice the pronunciation of *to*. Which is the strong form?

8.3   a. Who do I speak to?   b. Can I speak to John?

8.4 **2** Listen to the sentences. Which sound do you hear? Write a. or b.

Example   You can speak to him tomorrow.   *b.*

1 We're going to see him tomorrow.   ....

2 Did you listen to the news this morning? ....

3 Paolo is a man you can talk to.   ....

4 You can write to me at my office.   ....

5 You can talk to Paolo.   ....

6 What address do I write to?   ....

8.4 **3** Listen again and repeat the sentences.

Complete the rule.

• Use the .... form of *to* when the word is at the end of a sentence.

4 Match the questions and answers. Then practise the pronunciation in pairs.

Who did you talk to?   I listened to the news.
What did you listen to?   I walked to the office.
Who did you write to?   I talked to Paolo.
Where did you walk to?   I wrote to the boss.

6 Work in pairs. Ask your partner questions about future travel plans. Complete the market research survey form on travel.

Examples *Are you going to make any business trips in the next six months?*
Where are you going?
How are you going to travel?
How long are you going to stay?

MARKET RESEARCH SURVEY Future travel plans

	Where?	When?	How?	How long?
Business trips				
Holiday travel				
Social activities/ visits				

7 Work in groups. You have won a three-day holiday in Vienna. Look at the information on Vienna. Make a detailed plan of what you are going to do each day. Present your plan to another group.

Congratulations!

on winning a city break holiday to Vienna!
We have pleasure in enclosing details of your
flight and hotel, and some information on
places to visit in Vienna.

Flights

Out: Thursday 5 June OS 453 arrives 11.50.
Return: Sunday 8 June OS 454 departs 18.20.

Hotel

Half-board accommodation at the five-star
Ambassador Hotel from Thursday 5 June
until midday on Sunday 8 June.

What to do in *Vienna*

Places to visit

Albertina
World-famous graphic art collection. Drawings by Michelangelo, Raphael, Rembrandt, Rubens, Dürer, Schiele, Matisse, Picasso.
Mon–Thu 10–4 p.m., Fri–Sun 10–1 p.m.

Belvedere Palace: Austrian Gallery
19th and 20th century Austrian art, art nouveau, Klimt, Schiele, Kokoschka.
Tue–Sun 10–5 p.m.
Underground: U1, U4 Karlsplatz.

Hofburg Imperial Palace
State Rooms, Spanish Riding School.
Mon–Sat 8.30–4.30 p.m., Sun 8.30–1 p.m.

Museum of Fine Arts
Egyptian, Oriental, Greek, and Roman antiquities. Dutch, Flemish, Italian paintings. Master collection of paintings by Bruegel.
Tue–Fri 10–2 p.m., Sat–Sun 9–1 p.m.

Museum of Natural History
Wed–Mon 9–6 p.m.

Schönbrunn Palace and Park
Baroque palace with 1,441 rooms.
Palace guided tours daily 8.30–4.30 p.m.
Park daily 6 a.m. until dusk
Zoo daily 9.30–6.30 p.m.
Underground: U4 Schönbrunn.

St. Stephen's Cathedral
Guided tours Mon–Sat 10.30 a.m. and 3 p.m., Sat 7 p.m.

The Prater
View Vienna from the top of the Giant Ferris Wheel, built for the 1897 Vienna 'World Expo' and famous as the location of the film, *The Third Man*, starring Orson Welles.
9–11 p.m. Underground: U1 Praterstern/Wien Nord.

Things to do

Danube boat trips
Three-hour round trips leave from the Danube Canal. See Otto Wagner's art nouveau architecture, Hundertwasser's house, and UNO City. Price $18. Danube Canal Promenade.
Underground: U4 Schewedenplatz.

Vienna State Opera
Der Rosenkavalier, Strauss	Thu 7 p.m.
The Magic Flute, Mozart	Fri 6.30 p.m.
Aida, Verdi	Sat 7.30 p.m.

Nightlife
The Bermuda Triangle
Vienna's oldest quarter and liveliest night-spot. Live music, bars, restaurants, cafés. Many stay open until 4 a.m.
Underground: U4 Schewedenplatz.

Viennese *heuriger*
Enjoy an evening with Viennese wine, food, and songs, in traditional 'heuriger' taverns in Vienna's wine-growing suburbs.

Air travel file. Word map

1 Complete the word map on air travel below. Use your dictionary to check the meaning of new words.

passport control	seat-belt	trolley	customs
duty-free shop	information desk	life-jacket	suitcase
ticket	security check	arrivals board	window seat
boarding card	overhead locker	flight attendant	briefcase

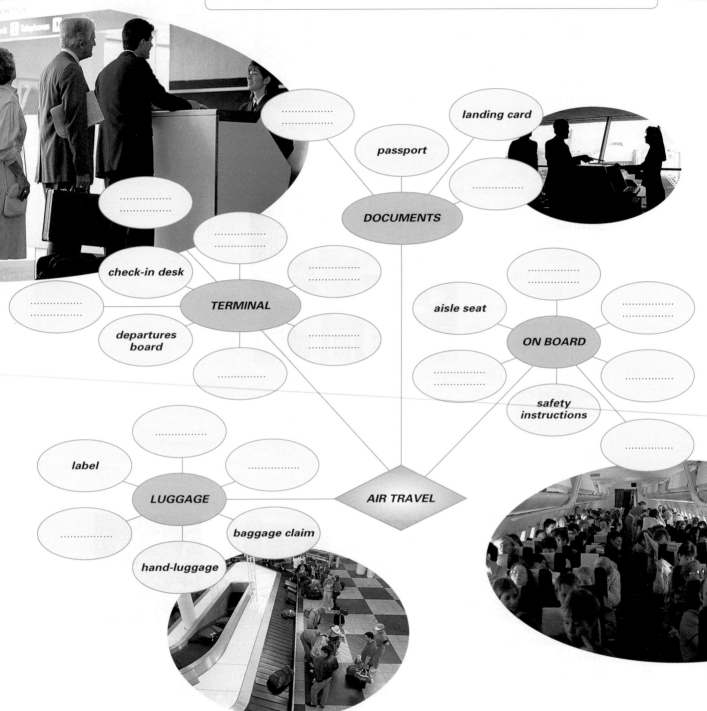

2 Work in groups. One student chooses a word from the word map. The other students ask questions to guess the word. The student who answers the questions can only give 'Yes' and 'No' answers.

Examples   *Is it a person?*
Is it a place inside an airport terminal?
Do I need it to travel by plane?
Is it important for safety reasons?

Flight announcements

1 Work in groups. Complete the airport information with the names and nationalities of the airlines.

Flight	Airline	Nationality
AF 645	....	....
AZ 1420	....	....
MA 732	Malev	Hungarian
LH 4980	....	....
IB 3765	Iberia	....
OA 287	Olympic	....

 Pocket Book p. 28

2 Do you normally hear the sentences below at the check-in desk (C), on the plane (P), or at the arrivals and customs area (A)? Tick C, P, or A.

	C	P	A
1 Would you like some more tea or coffee?			
2 Smoking or non-smoking?			
3 Please extinguish all cigarettes.			
4 Did you pack your bags yourself?			
5 Have you left your suitcase unattended at any time?			
6 Would you open your briefcase, please?			
7 Do you have any hand-luggage?			
8 Do you have more than the duty-free allowance?			

8.5 **3** Listen to the flight announcements. Complete the air travel information below.

Flight No.	Time	Destination	Information	Gate
AF 962	11.15	Marseilles	....	....
LH 4037	11.25	Dusseldorf	....	....
IB 3915	....	Malaga	....	10
AZ	11.45	Venice	LAST CALL	....
OA	11.45	Athens	LAST CALL	....

8.6 **4** Listen to five more airport announcements. Number the descriptions below 1–5 in the order you hear the announcements.

a. a general announcement about boarding ☐

b. a request to a passenger ☐

c. a last call to a specific passenger ☐

d. a security announcement to one passenger ☐

e. a general security announcement ☐

5 Match A and B to make the in-flight announcements.

A

1 Please fasten
2 Smoking is not allowed
3 Please make sure your seat
4 We will shortly be serving
5 Non-EU passengers are required
6 Please remain seated until

B

a. drinks and a light meal.
b. in rows 1 to 6 and 10 to 22, and in the toilets.
c. to fill in a landing card.
d. your seat-belts.
e. the aircraft has come to a complete standstill.
f. is in the upright position for take-off.

8.7 **6** Listen and check your answers.

7 Find the word or phrase in 5 above which means the same as

1 soon
2 must
3 stay in your seats
4 in the vertical position
5 to complete
6 has stopped

8 Work in groups. Choose a topic. Answer five questions from your colleagues on that topic.

- My experience of flying
- Why I fly/don't fly
- My worst journey
- Airports I like or dislike

9 Project. Prepare a short talk, or write a short article for your company newsletter on one of the topics below.

- Changes in air travel in the last fifty years
- The best airline

Invitations

8.8 **1** Read the invitation. Listen to the telephone conversation between Monique Bresson and Duncan Ross. Answer the questions.

1 What invitation does Duncan make on the phone?
2 What is Monique's response?

Monique Bresson is invited to the 10th anniversary celebration of *Wine and Dine* magazine, to take place on Saturday 14 and Sunday 15 June at Glencross Castle, Scotland.

m Return flight London–Edinburgh by charter aircraft is included in this invitation.
Duncan Ross
Editor and Publisher *Wine and Dine* magazine
RSVP 15 Honeywell Street, London EC4 1DT

8.9 **2** After talking to Monique, Duncan phones James Turner. Listen to their conversation. Answer the questions.

1 Why doesn't James accept Duncan's invitation?
2 What makes him change his mind?

8.8, 8.9 **3** Listen to both telephone conversations again. Tick the phrases you hear.

Inviting
I'd like to invite you to…
Would you join us…?
Would you like to…?
Why don't you…?
How about…?

Accepting
Thank you. I'd be delighted to accept.
Thank you. I'd love to.
Thank you. I'd enjoy that.

Declining
I'd love to, but (*I'm afraid I can't*).
Thanks a lot, but (*I've made another arrangement*).

4 Role-play. Work in pairs. Use the phrases in 3 above to make and respond to invitations. Think of two more situations and practise them.

	Student A	Student B
Situation 1		
	Invite your colleague to join you for lunch tomorrow.	
		Decline and give a reason.
	Suggest another day next week.	
		Accept.
Situation 2		
		Invite your colleague for a drink after work.
	Decline and give a reason. Suggest lunch another day.	
		Accept.

REVIEW UNIT B

This unit reviews all the main language points from units 5–8. Complete the exercises. Check your learning with the Self-check box at the end.

1   **Mass and count nouns.** *Some/any/a lot (of)/much/many*

Five of the sentences below have a grammatical mistake. Find the mistakes. Write the correct sentences.

1 Could you give me an information, please?
2 Would you like some wine?
3 I didn't buy much fruit.
4 He gave me some useful advices.
5 The news is not very good.
6 I did a lot of exercises at the gym.
7 How many money did you spend?
8 I haven't got some paper.
9 Many people attended the conference.
10 He has much experience in marketing.

2   *Some/any/a lot (of)/much/many*

Work in pairs. Find out about your partner's home town.
Ask about

restaurants	Examples *Is/Are there any...?*
historical buildings	*Is there much...?*
parks	*Are there many...?*
industry	*Yes, there is/are some/a lot.*
open space	*No, there isn't much.*
unemployment	*Yes, there are.*
nightlife	
famous sights	
good hotels	
traffic jams	

❸ Present Perfect Simple questions with *ever*

Work in pairs. Ask your partner questions in the Present Perfect Simple with *ever*. If your partner answers *Yes, I have*, ask for more details. Add three more questions.

Example   **Student A**   *Have you ever been to America?*
              Student B   *Yes, I have.*
              Student A   *When was that? How long was the flight?*

Student A

Ask Student B	Yes	No	Details
1 (be) on a holiday in the mountains?			
2 (have) an accident?			
3 (miss) a flight?			
4 (work) in another country?			
5 (lose) something important or valuable?			
6			
7			
8			

Student B

Ask Student A	Yes	No	Details
1 (be) on a city sightseeing holiday?			
2 (have) a bad experience while travelling?			
3 (study or work) all night?			
4 (meet) a famous person?			
5 (want) to live in another country?			
6			
7			
8			

❹ Past Simple, Present Perfect Simple, and Present Perfect Continuous

Find the grammatical mistake in each of these sentences. Write the correct sentence.

1 I haven't seen him since ages.
2 How long ago have you had a holiday?
3 How long are they married?
4 I've had my present job since a long time.
5 Have you ever gone to Canada?
6 How many candidates have you been interviewing today?
7 She's changed her job a month ago.
8 How long are you working for your present company?
9 He's changed jobs twice last year.
10 She studies Japanese since 1993.

❺ Present, Past, or Present Perfect Simple?

Complete the text with the correct form of the verb in brackets.

Manuel Gomez _____ ¹(be) at UltraTech Inc. since he _____ ²(leave) college. Since he _____ ³(join) the company, he _____ ⁴(work) in three different departments. In his present job in the Sales Department, he usually _____ ⁵ (travel) to Switzerland every two or three months. Last year he _____ ⁶(be) also responsible for Southern Europe, and he _____ ⁷(go) to Spain and Italy on business five times.

He _____ ⁸(not go) to Spain so far this year. At the moment, he _____ ⁹(be) in Thailand on holiday with his wife and daughter. It _____ ¹⁰(be) their first trip; they _____ ¹¹(never, visit) the Far East before. They _____ ¹²(fly) from London last week and they _____ ¹³(visit) many of Bangkok's interesting sights this week.

6 Present Perfect Simple or Continuous?

Complete these sentences with the Present Perfect Simple or Continuous.

1 You .... (drink) six cups of coffee since lunch-time!

2 We .... (drink) coffee all afternoon.

3 She .... (type) all the letters and I .... (sign) them all.

4 He .... (play) in every match this season.

5 They look very tired. They .... (walk) for hours without a break.

6 She .... (lose) her pen. She .... (look) for it all day.

7 Futures: Present Continuous or *going to*?

Work in pairs. Make sentences with *going to* or the Present Continuous to describe your arrangements, plans, or intentions for next weekend.

Example   Student A *What are you going to do next Saturday morning?*
           Student B *I'm playing golf at nine in the morning. After that,*
                      I'm going to sit in the garden and read a good book.

8 Making and changing arrangements

Work in pairs. Practise making and changing arrangements.

Student A

Phone B and ask for a meeting.

Student B

Say 'yes'. Ask when.

Suggest a day.

Apologize and say 'no'.
Suggest another day.

Say 'yes'.

End the conversation.

Student B

Phone A to change the meeting date.

Student A

Ask when B is free.

Suggest two dates.

Choose a date.

Say 'yes'. End the conversation.

9 Inviting

Work in pairs. Write a short conversation for each of the following situations. Practise the conversations with a partner.

Situation 1
Sue phones Mike to invite him to a party. Mike declines and gives the reason.

Situation 2
Mike phones Sue to invite her to the theatre. Sue accepts.

Situation 3
James Turner phones Monique Bresson. He invites her to travel to Scotland with him to Duncan Ross's anniversary celebration. (You decide on Monique's answer.)

⑩ Making suggestions

Work in pairs. Plan some activities for next week. Suggest, accept, or reject the following activities. If you don't like the suggestion, give an alternative activity. Add two more suggestions.

Student A	Student B
1 a walk in the country	1 a concert
2 a visit to an exhibition	2 a party for a friend's birthday
3 a boat trip on the river	3 dinner at a good restaurant
4 a game of tennis	4 a theatre visit
5	5 ....

Example   **Student A** *How about going to a museum on Monday afternoon?*
                Student B *Yes, fine. What about having an Italian meal in the evening?*

⑪ Giving opinions, agreeing, and disagreeing

Work in pairs. Practise asking and giving opinions. Agree or disagree with your partner's opinion. Ask about

1 a famous film star		4 a capital city	
2 a sport		5 a national cuisine	
3 a holiday destination		6 a famous politician	

Example   **Student A** *In my opinion, Paris is the most interesting capital city in Europe. What do you think?*
                Student B *I don't agree. I think Amsterdam is.*

⑫ Restaurant language

Work in groups. Write out a simple local menu. Practise describing the dishes, asking for and making recommendations.

⑬ Vocabulary

Work in two groups, A and B. Write a vocabulary test to give to the other group. Choose ten of the words below. Write a sentence or phrase to help the other group guess each word.

Example   Word *surplus*
               Clue   *the opposite of deficit*

cruise	employee	decade	~~surplus~~	luggage
candidate	trainee	briefcase	security	advice
delay	safety	suitcase	flight	passenger
aisle seat	abroad	fare	consumer	disorganized

⑭ Vocabulary test

Give your vocabulary test to the other group. Return the test for checking.

Look at the self-check box below. Tick the areas you need to review again.

SELF-CHECK BOX	Yes	No	Pocket Book
● Mass and count nouns *some/any/a lot of/much/many*			6
● Present and Past Simple			2, 4
● Present Perfect Simple, *ever*			7
● Present Perfect Continuous			8
● Futures: Present Continuous, *going to*			3, 9
● Making/changing arrangements			20
● Inviting			21
● Making suggestions			20
● Opinions/agreeing/disagreeing			20
● Vocabulary			

UNIT 9
Europe's high-speed future

Language focus ❶ Have you ever travelled on a high-speed train? Read the extracts from an article about six high-speed trains. Note one interesting fact about each of the six trains.

The Japanese began the race for high speeds in 1964 with the first 210kph *Shinkansen* between Tokyo and Osaka. Today Japan's 300 high-speed trains carry 355,000 passengers daily, at speeds of 265kph.

One of the long-term benefits of Expo'92 in Seville is the AVE which travels between Madrid and Seville. It has reduced the journey from seven and a half to two and a half hours.

France leads on speed, with high-speed trains reaching 300kph. The Paris–Lyon line has been so successful that double-decker TGVs now operate on that route. The French plan to have a 4,200km rail network by the year 2025. Their trains will reach commercial speeds of 350kph.

Italy operates the 250kph *Pendolino* trains on the Florence–Rome, Milan–Rome, and Rome–Naples routes. This train gets its name from the way it tilts to go round curves faster.

Sweden also chose tilting trains. Their X2000s cut the four-hour Stockholm–Gothenburg journey to three hours. A survey has shown that the X2000 is the most popular form of transport for 96% of travellers on this route.

German Railways has put a lot of money into the technically complex ICEs, which started operating in 1991 on the Hamburg–Munich route. They offer extensive facilities for the business user, including phone, fax, photocopier, and PC terminal.

2 Read the article about European train travel in the next century. Answer the questions.

1 What is the CER proposal?
2 When did the first TGV line start operating?
3 What effect have high-speed trains had on airlines on many routes?

THE NEW AGE OF THE TRAIN

In January 1989, the Community of European Railways (CER) presented their proposal for a high-speed, pan-European train network, extending from Sweden to Sicily, and from Portugal to Poland, by the year 2020. If their proposal becomes a reality, it will revolutionize train travel in Europe. Journeys between major cities will take half the time they take today. Brussels will be only one and a half hours from Paris. The quickest way to get from Paris to Frankfurt, from Milan to Marseilles, and from Barcelona to Madrid, will be by train, not plane.

When the network is complete, it will integrate three types of railway line: totally new high-speed lines with trains operating at speeds of 300kph; upgraded lines, which allow for speeds up to 200-225kph; and existing lines, for local connections and distribution of freight.

'If business people can choose between a three-hour train journey from city centre to city centre, and a one-hour flight, they'll choose the train,' says an executive travel consultant. 'They won't go by plane any more. If you calculate flight time, check-in, and travel to and from the airport, you'll find almost no difference. And if your plane arrives late, due to bad weather or air traffic congestion or strikes, then the train passengers will arrive at their destination first!'

Since France introduced the first 260kph TGV service between Paris and Lyon in 1981, the trains have achieved higher and higher speeds. On many routes, airlines have lost up to 90% of their passengers to high-speed trains. If people accept the CER's plan, the 21st century will be 'The New Age of the Train'.

3 Underline five verbs in the text which refer to the future.

Future: *will,* 1st Conditional, *if* and *when*

Read the examples. Complete the grammar rules.

will
- Journeys between major cities **will take** half the time they take today.
- Brussels **will be** only one and a half hours from Paris.
- They **won't go** by plane any more.

● Use .... + infinitive to predict future situations and actions.

How do we make questions and short answers with *will* + infinitive?

 Pocket Book p. 10

Note *will* becomes *'ll* in spoken English, except in short answers.
      will not becomes *won't* in spoken English.

1st Conditional
- **If** their proposal **becomes** a reality, it **will revolutionize** train travel in Europe.
- **If** people **accept** the CER's plan, the 21st century **will be** 'The New Age of the Train'.

● To make the 1st Conditional, use *if* + the .... , + *will* + infinitive.

● Use the .... to express a future possibility and its result.

if and *when*
- **If** your plane arrives late, the train passengers will arrive at their destination first!
- **When** the network is complete, it will integrate three types of railway lines.

● Use *if* to express a possibility and .... to express a certainty.

 Pocket Book p. 11

Practice ❶ Write the questions for these answers. The information you need is in the article, *The New Age of the Train.*

Example *How far will the network extend?*
It will extend from Sweden to Sicily, and from Portugal to Poland.

1 How long .... ?
They will take half the time they take today.

2 How long .... ?
It will take one and a half hours.

3 How many .... ?
There will be three different types of line.

4 Which method of travel .... ?
They will choose the train.

5 What .... ?
It will be 'The New Age of the Train' in the writer's opinion.

Pronunciation ① Listen to the examples on the tape. What is the difference in the vowel sounds underlined?

9.1 ▭ a. pr<u>i</u>nter   b. Sw<u>e</u>den

9.2 ▭ ② Listen to the tape. Which sound do you hear? Write a. or b.

Example will *a.*

1 ....   3 ....   5 ....   7 ....

2 ....   4 ....   6 ....   8 ....

9.2 ▭ ③ Listen again and repeat the words.

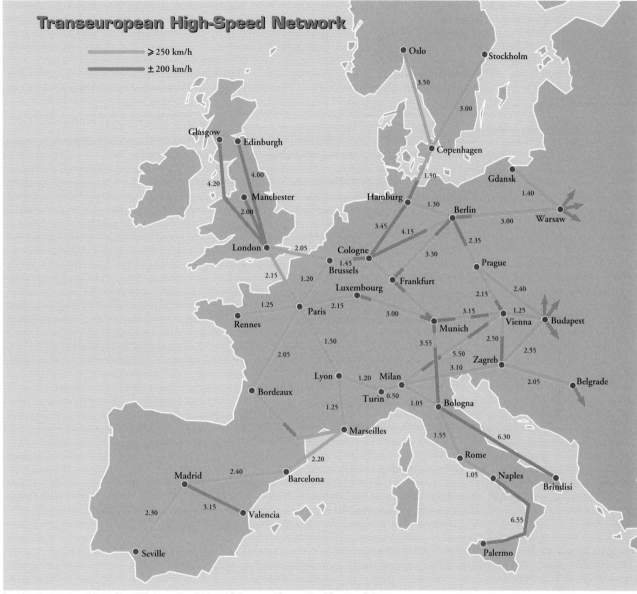

Transeuropean High-Speed Network

Based on the Long-term Master Plan 1992, International Union of Railways and Community of European Railways.

2 Work in pairs. You want to know about train journey times in the future. Look at the map and ask and answer questions. Ask about three journeys each.

Examples *How long will the journey from Paris to Luxembourg take?*
It'll take two and a quarter hours.
How fast will trains travel on that line?
They'll travel at 250kph.

3 Work in pairs. Ask and answer questions about your future. Write notes on your partner's answers. Ask two more questions.

Examples *Do you think you will start a business some day?*
Yes, definitely!/No, definitely not!
I think so./I don't think so.
I hope so./I hope not.

Student A	Student B
1 buy/new car/next year	1 work/another country/in the next five years
2 change/job/soon	2 learn/more English/next year
3 move/house/next three years	3 begin/new sport or hobby/future
4 learn/another language/future	4 go/world cruise/next five years
5 have/holiday in the UK or USA/ next year	5 have/holiday/Australia or Far East/next year.
6	6 ....
7	7 ....

UNIT 9 ● 83

4 Make predictions about changes in your organization or your country. Give your reasons.

Example   *I think my organization will/won't grow because I'm sure the present government will/won't cut taxes.*

Your organization
1 make/profit/next year
2 do/more business/other countries
3 spend/less money/training
4 recruit/more people/next two years
5 invest/more money/new technology

Your country
1 present government/win the next election
2 unemployment/decrease
3 economic situation/get worse
4 taxes/stay at the same level
5 exports/increase

5 Complete the sentences with your own ideas.

Examples   If exports increase, *the economic situation will improve.*
The government will lose popularity *if they increase taxes.*

1 If more companies close down, ...

2 If taxes go up, ...

3 Unemployment will decrease if ....

4 Exports will increase if ....

5 If the present government loses the next election, ...

....

6 If my company expands, ...

7 If I get a big salary increase, ...

8 I will look for another job if ....

9 If another company offers me a job at twice my present salary, ...

....

10 If my company makes a big loss, ...

6 You have an important business trip to South America next week. What will you do if things go wrong? Make sentences from the information below.

Example   *If I become ill, I'll cancel my trip.*

What will you do if

1 your car breaks down on the way to the airport?
2 you lose your plane ticket?
3 you lose your passport?
4 the airline loses your suitcase?
5 someone steals your wallet?
6 you lose your voice?
7 you miss your plane home?

7 Describe your plans for tomorrow. Say what you will do if things go wrong.

Example   *I'm meeting a customer tomorrow. If the meeting isn't successful, we won't sign the contract.*

8 Work in groups. Discuss these questions. Give reasons for your opinions.

1 Do you think the 21st century will be 'The New Age of the Train'? What will this depend on?
2 If the CER proposal becomes a reality, will more people prefer to travel by train than by plane?
3 Will Europe solve its traffic problems if it has an integrated network of high-speed trains?
4 What other changes will there be in the way people travel in the next century?

Train travel file. Collocations.

1 Work in pairs. Look at the signs from a railway station or train.

Which sign shows you where you can
1 get some information about train times?
2 leave a suitcase for a few hours?
3 buy a ticket?
4 ask about an umbrella you left on a train?
5 sit down and read a book until your train leaves?
6 get on a train?
7 see the platform a train will leave from?
8 have a coffee and a sandwich?
9 make a complaint?

2 Complete the compounds with words from the box.

| monthly |
| underground |
| train |
| period return |
| intercity |
| taxi |
| annual |
| plane |
| day return |

bus

....
.... fare
....

single

....
.... ticket
off-peak return

weekly

.... season ticket
....

....
commuter trains

3 Complete the grid to show which verbs we use with these forms of transport.

	plane	train	bus	coach	car	taxi	bicycle	motorbike
to catch/miss		✓		✓				
to drive								
to ride								
to get on/off				✓				
to get into/out of								
to take								

4 Rail transport survey. Work in two groups. Prepare a questionnaire to find out about train travel. Interview a colleague from the other group with your questionnaire. Ask questions to find out

● how people usually travel.
● how often they travel by train (underground, commuter, intercity).
● which types of ticket they buy.
● their opinion about fares (cheap, reasonable, over-priced).
● their suggestions for improving the rail services.

The electronic personal assistant

1 Read the text about the Newton MessagePad. Which computer application do you think is the most useful?

The Newton MessagePad

The astonishing new invention that has room for your whole world but fits in your pocket.

The Newton MessagePad communications assistant is the first in a family of products from Apple Computer that uses a revolutionary new technology called Newton Intelligence. This technology makes it possible for the MessagePad not only to recognize handwriting and graphics, but also to understand the things people do every day – make phone calls, write letters, and schedule meetings – and then it helps them to do these things.

It has four built-in, completely integrated pieces of computer software applications: a Notepad; a To Do list; a Name File; finally, a Date Book.

Newton keeps information on your colleagues and friends. If you don't remember them all, Newton will.

Newton helps you plan your daily, weekly, and monthly schedules.

Newton reminds you of everything you plan to do.

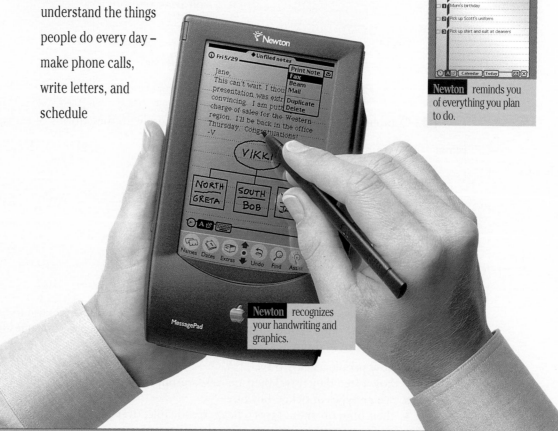

Newton recognizes your handwriting and graphics.

9.3  **2** Listen to Clive Girling, Product Marketing Manager for Apple Computer UK. He is giving a briefing about the Newton MessagePad. Answer the questions.

1 Why is the Newton MessagePad very easy to use?
2 How can you use the Newton to communicate with other people?
3 Can you use other software with the Newton?

3 Work in groups. Prepare ten questions to find out if there is a market for the Newton MessagePad. Find out what systems people use to organize their notes, appointments, addresses, birthdays, etc. Find out if they think the Newton MessagePad will be useful for them.

4 Work in pairs. Interview a colleague from a different group, using the ten questions. Make a note of your colleague's answers.

5 Work in the same group as in 3. Decide if there is a market for the Newton MessagePad. Present your opinions and reasons to the class.

6 Project. Work in groups. Design your own small computer. Discuss

- appearance, size, weight, colour
- price
- applications that would be useful
- markets

Present your ideas to the class.

Offers and requests

9.4 🔘 **1** Listen to a conversation between Duncan Ross and his secretary, Carol. Write down what Duncan wants Carol to do.

Book flight ....

Book hotel ....

Get information about ....

9.5 🔘 **2** Listen to another conversation between Duncan and his secretary later the same day. Answer the questions.

1 How does Duncan want to travel back to London?
2 Why doesn't he need a hotel in Bordeaux?

9.4, 9.5 🔘 **3** Listen to the two conversations again and tick the phrases you hear.

Requesting
Can you...?
Could you...?

Do you mind...(+ -*ing*)?
Would you mind...(+ -*ing*)?

Would you...?
Do you think you could...?

Offering
Shall I...?
Do you want me to...?
If you like, I can...
Would you like me to...?

Agreeing
Yes, of course.
Yes, certainly.

Not at all.
No, of course not.

Refusing
I'm sorry, but that's not possible.
I'm afraid not.

Accepting
Yes, please.
Thank you.
That's very kind of you.
Thank you. I'd appreciate that.

Declining
Thanks, but please don't bother.
Thanks, but that won't be necessary.
That's very kind of you but...

4 Work in pairs.

Student A Student B is visiting your company. Practise making, accepting, and declining offers in these situations. Add two more situations.

Student B You are a visitor to Student A's company. Practise making, accepting, and declining offers in these situations. Add two more situations.

Student A	**Student B**
Offer	
1 to carry Student B's suitcase.	Decline.
2 to get him/her a drink.	Accept.
3 to show Student B round your company.	Accept.
4	....
5 to explain the programme you've arranged.	Accept.
6 to accompany Student B to his/her hotel.	Decline.
7 to order a taxi to his/her hotel.	Decline.
8	....

Now change roles.

5 Work in pairs. Practise making and responding to requests. Add two more requests.

Student A	**Student B**
Ask Student B to	
1 lend you his/her newspaper.	Agree.
2 look after a visitor tomorrow.	Refuse (you are out all day).
3 give you next year's budget.	Agree.
4	....

Student B	**Student A**
Ask Student A to	
5 give you a lift to the station.	Agree.
6 show you how a new computer works.	Refuse (you don't understand it yourself).
7 lend you a calculator.	Agree.
8	....

6 Work in pairs. Practise making offers and requests for these situations. Add more situations.

1 Offer to show a visitor round your city.
2 Offer to explain the menu in a restaurant to a foreign guest.
3 Ask a friend to lend you some money.
4 Ask a colleague for some advice.
5 Offer to book a hotel room for a visitor.
6 Ask a colleague to help you write a report.
7 Offer to take a visitor out to lunch.
8 Offer to help a colleague prepare a presentation.
9 Ask a friend to pick you up at the airport.

UNIT 10
Cities in crisis

▼AGENDA

▷ 2nd Conditional

▷ Prepositions of place file. Preposition diagrams

▷ Business correspondence

▷ Asking for information

Language focus ① What traffic problems do cities in your country have? What are the authorities doing about the problems?

② Work in pairs. Read the newspaper extracts about traffic in European cities. Make a list of the problems they refer to.

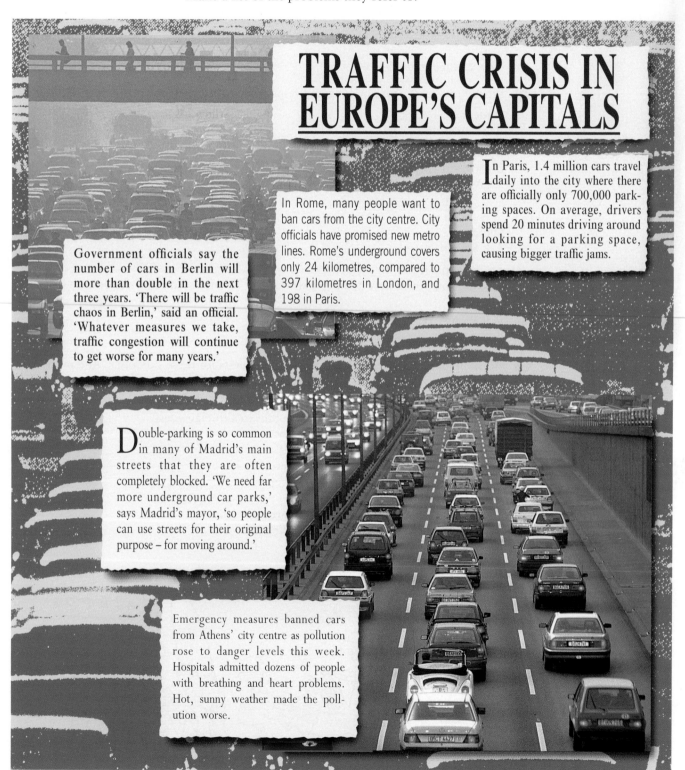

TRAFFIC CRISIS IN EUROPE'S CAPITALS

In Paris, 1.4 million cars travel daily into the city where there are officially only 700,000 parking spaces. On average, drivers spend 20 minutes driving around looking for a parking space, causing bigger traffic jams.

In Rome, many people want to ban cars from the city centre. City officials have promised new metro lines. Rome's underground covers only 24 kilometres, compared to 397 kilometres in London, and 198 in Paris.

Government officials say the number of cars in Berlin will more than double in the next three years. 'There will be traffic chaos in Berlin,' said an official. 'Whatever measures we take, traffic congestion will continue to get worse for many years.'

Double-parking is so common in many of Madrid's main streets that they are often completely blocked. 'We need far more underground car parks,' says Madrid's mayor, 'so people can use streets for their original purpose – for moving around.'

Emergency measures banned cars from Athens' city centre as pollution rose to danger levels this week. Hospitals admitted dozens of people with breathing and heart problems. Hot, sunny weather made the pollution worse.

10.1 🔊 **❸** Listen to an extract from a radio phone-in programme called *Viewpoint*. Four callers talk about traffic congestion. Write 1, 2, 3, or 4 next to the solution each caller suggests.

Caller

a. stop building motorways ....

b. charge motorists for driving in city centres ....

c. improve public transport in cities ....

d. ban cars completely from city centres ....

10.1 🔊 **❹** Listen to the extract again and tick T (true) or F (false).

	T	F
1 The first caller thinks people would drive less in cities if public transport were better.		
2 The second caller thinks if motorists paid a fee to drive in cities, they would use their cars less.		
3 The third caller believes if the government built more motorways, there would be less congestion.		
4 The fourth speaker believes people would be healthier if there were no cars in cities.		

2nd Conditional

Read the examples. Complete the grammar rules.

- If motorists **had to** pay to drive in cities, they **would use** their cars a lot less.
- If I **were** the Transport Minister, I **would stop** building motorways.
- We **could make** some of the money **if** we **charged** people for driving in cities.

- To make the 2nd Conditional, use *if* + Past Simple, + ... or *could* + infinitive.

- Use the 2nd Conditional to express an unlikely or unreal condition and its probable result in the present or future.

  Is it also correct to say *If I was the Transport Minister...*

  What is the difference in meaning between these sentences?
  If I have more time, I'll travel more.
  If I had more time, I'd travel more.

Pocket Book p. 12

Practice **❶** Complete the sentences with your own ideas.

1 If motorists had to pay to drive in city centres, ...

2 People wouldn't use their cars so much in cities if ....

3 If public transport were free, ...

4 Roads and motorways would not be so crowded if ....

5 The air in our cities would be cleaner if ....

6 If we banned cars in city centres, ...

7 If we stopped building motorways, ...

8 People would be healthier if ....

❷ Describe three things you would do if you were the Transport Minister in your country.

3 Work in pairs. Compare your answers to these questions.

1 If you could have any car, which would you choose?
2 If you didn't need to study English, which language would you learn?
3 If you had time to begin a new sport or hobby, which would you choose?
4 If you could change your job, which job would you choose?
5 If you were ten years younger, would you change your life in any way?

4 Answer the questions.

What would you do
1 if your boss wanted you to spend your summer holiday attending a full-time English course in the UK?
2 if your company offered you a job with a higher salary but longer hours, and three months' travel a year?
3 if you had £10,000 to spend on your department?
4 if your company asked you to work in Japan or America for two years?
5 if your organization gave you three months' paid holiday to spend as you liked?

5 Work in pairs. Write six more questions to complete this questionnaire. Then interview another colleague. Make a note of the answers.

My idea of a perfect weekend

Name ....

Answers

1 Where would you go? ....
2 How would you get there? ....
3 Where would you stay? ....
4 What essential object would you take? ....
5 ....
6 ....
7 ....
8 ....
9 ....
10 ....

Pronunciation

10.2

1 Listen to the sentences. Which words are stressed?

a. I'd do more sport if I had enough time.
b. If I earned more money, I'd buy a new car.

2 Mark the most important words in these sentences.

1 If I had a car, I'd drive it to work.
2 If I lived in the city, I'd travel by bike.
3 I'd take more exercise if I were you.
4 If they banned all cars, the air would be cleaner.
5 If the buses were quicker, more people would use them.
6 Would you take the train if you could?

10.3 **3** Listen and check your answers. Then listen and repeat.

4 Work in pairs. Ask and answer questions. Begin like this.

Where would you go if...?
Would you buy a new car if...?
What would you do if...?
Would you take your car if...?

Prepositions of place file. Preposition diagrams

1 Look at the photo of an office. Write the correct number in the key.

Key
- [ ] ashtray
- [ ] diary
- [ ] phone
- [ ] bookcase
- [ ] filing cabinet
- [ ] table lamp
- [ ] chair
- [ ] table
- [ ] desk
- [ ] clock
- [ ] keyboard
- [ ] photocopier
- [ ] bin
- [ ] coffee machine
- [ ] year planner
- [ ] computer
- [ ] mouse
- [ ] mineral water

2 Describe the location of objects in the office. Use the prepositions in the diagrams.
Examples   *The table is under the photocopier.*
            The clock is above the year planner.

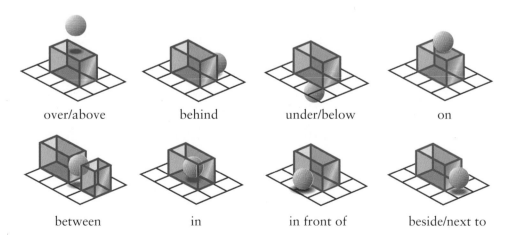

over/above   behind   under/below   on

between   in   in front of   beside/next to

3 Work in pairs. Describe your office or a room in your home to your partner. Draw the room your partner describes. Do not show your partner the drawing until you have finished.

Business correspondence

1 Work in pairs. Read these statements about letters. Tick if they are T (true) or F (false).

Letter-writing quiz	T	F
1 If a letter begins with the receiver's name, e.g. *Dear Mr Thorn*, it closes with *Yours sincerely* and the signature.		
2 If you wrote to Peter Burt and wanted to use his first name, you would write *Dear Mr Peter*.		
3 If you did not know if a female correspondent was married or not, you could write *Ms*, instead of *Miss* or *Mrs*.		
4 If you wrote a letter to Mrs Susan Lambert, you would open with *Dear Mrs Susan Lambert*.		
5 The abbreviation for a doctor is Dt, e.g. *Dear Dt Bell*.		
6 If you did not know the receiver's name, you would close the letter with *Yours faithfully* and the signature.		
7 In the USA, the date 5/8/96 on a letter means 8 May 1996.		
8 It is correct to begin a letter with *Gentlemen* in the USA.		

Check your answers.

 Pocket Book p. 24, 25, 26

2 Business letters use standard phrases, for example, for requesting, confirming, asking for information, and thanking. Read the letter and underline the standard word or phrase for

1 enclosing documents
2 finishing the letter
3 making reference to previous contact
4 starting to give bad news

Ms Viner
Flat 6c
14 Brunswick Road
Edinburgh

22 January

Tour France

118 St Patrick's Road,
London WIR OAW
tel: 0171 234 9487

Dear Ms Viner

With reference to your telephone call today, we have pleasure in enclosing some information about organized tours of the wine regions of France.

Unfortunately, the booklet you requested, *The Wine Regions of France*, is currently out of stock. We will send you a copy as soon as new stocks arrive.

Please contact us again if you would like any further information.

Yours sincerely

Jean Perrin

Jean Perrin
Tourist Information Officer

3 Work in pairs. Match the phrases to the function they express.

Functions	Standard phrases
1 Making reference	a. Could you possibly...?
2 Explaining the reason for writing	b. I am afraid that...
3 Requesting	c. With reference to your letter of 20 February...
4 Enclosing documents	d. Please find enclosed...
5 Confirming	e. I am writing to enquire about...
6 Giving bad news	f. Please contact us again if we can help in any way.
7 Thanking	g. We apologize for the mistake.
8 Apologizing	h. Thank you very much for sending...
9 Referring to future contact	i. I am pleased to confirm that...
10 Finishing the letter	j. I look forward to seeing you next month.

4 Complete the letter with suitable phrases.

INSTITUTE OF ENERGY CONSERVATION

51 St John's Street, Manchester M1 4DF

Prof. J. Penn
19A Gloucester St
Faringdon
OXON OSN 7JA

21 March

Dear John

.... [1] to ask you if you could make a presentation of your latest research at our annual conference next month.

.... [2] a provisional programme, to give you an idea of the main topics, and details of the conference hotel.

.... [3] not writing to ask you earlier, and I very much hope that you will be able to talk to us.

.... [4].

With best wishes
Yours sincerely

Marcus Lerner

Dr Marcus Lerner
Director

5 Work in pairs. Write a letter of reply to Dr Marcus Lerner. Agree to his request. Include these functions in your letter.

1 Making reference
2 Thanking
3 Confirming
4 Requesting
5 Finishing the letter

6 Project. You want to attend an English course in Britain. Write a letter to the British Council, Medlock St, Manchester M15 4AA. Describe the type of course you are interested in and request information and advice.

Asking for information

10.4 ❶   Duncan Ross's secretary, Carol, phones British Airways reservations office to get information about flights. Listen to the conversation. Note down the times of flights.

Flight times			
Sun p.m.	Edinburgh	–	Paris
Fri	Bordeaux	–	London

10.4 ❷   Listen to the conversation again and tick the phrases you hear.

Asking for information
I'd like | some information about…
         | to know…
Do you know?
Can you tell me?
Could you tell me?

Showing understanding
I see.
Right, I've got that.
So…

Checking
Let me check.
I'll look that up.

Apologizing
I'm afraid I don't have any information about…
I'm sorry, I can't tell you…

Asking for repetition
Could you repeat that, please?
Could you say that again?

10.5 ❸   Carol phones French Railways in London. Listen to the conversation and note down the information.

Train times	Paris	Bordeaux
Wed arrive by 1 p.m.		
Which station?		

10.5 ❹   Listen to the conversation again and complete the questions.

1 Can you tell me when .... ?

2 Could you tell me when .... ?

3 Do you know which station .... ?

❺   Compare the questions from the two conversations. Which are more polite, the direct or indirect questions? What is the difference in the form of the verb?

Direct questions
What time **does** the direct flight **arrive?**
When **do** the later flights **arrive?**
Do I **need** to make a reservation?

Indirect questions
Do you know if Air France **flies** from Bordeaux to London?
Can you tell me when you **want** to travel?
Could you tell me when it **leaves?**
Do you know which station it **leaves** from?

❻   Work in pairs. Some of these questions are not correct. Write the correct question.

1 Could you tell me what the fare is?
2 I'd like to know how long does the journey take.
3 Do you know if there's a dining car on the train?
4 Can you tell me which airport does the flight leave from?
5 Do you know how much is the fare?
6 I'd like to know where can I buy a ticket.

7 Work in pairs. Ask for and give information. Practise asking indirect questions.
Begin your questions with the phrases in 2 above.

Role-play 1

Student A
Phone British Airways. Ask for
information about flights from
London Heathrow to Madrid.

You want to know

- how many flights a day
- when flights depart/arrive
- what/cheapest fare
- if/any restrictions/on cheapest fare

Student B
You work for British Airways.
Use the information below to
answer an enquiry.

British Airways Flight Information			
From London Heathrow to Madrid			
	Depart	**Arrive**	**Flight number**
Daily	0830	1145	BA 458
	1410	1725	BA 460
	1910	2225	BA 462
Fares	Club Europe		£480
	Euro Traveller full economy fare		£234
	*Apex economy fare		£135

* Apex fares must include a Saturday night stay and must be booked
a minimum of seven days in advance.

Role-play 2

Student A
You work for French Railways
in London. Use the information
below to answer an enquiry.

Student B
Phone French Railways. Ask for
information about trains from
Paris to Frankfurt.

You want to know

- how many trains a day
- when trains/depart/arrive
- how much/1st and 2nd class fares

FRENCH RAILWAYS			
	EC 57 **1**	**EC 55** **2**	**EC 53** **3**
Paris–Est	08.55	12.58	17.14
Metz	11.52	15.55	20.02
Mannheim	14.11	18.11	22.19
Frankfurt/Main	15.06	19.06	23.15

Notes

1	Daily	EC	Heinrich Heine	X
2	Daily	EC	Gustav Eiffel	X
3	Daily	EC	Goethe	X (Supplement on certain days)

Fares	**1st class**	**2nd class**
Single	£95	£64
Return	£190	£128

UNIT 11
Communicating across cultures

Language focus ❶ Are these statements true about social customs in your country? Tick **Yes**, **No**, or **It depends**.

	Yes	No	It depends
a. People shake hands when they meet for the first time and when they meet after a long time. Colleagues don't shake hands every day.			
b. In a professional situation people usually exchange business cards at a first meeting.			
c. It's very important to arrive punctually for a professional meeting.			
d. Colleagues generally use first names at work.			
e. People prefer to keep their work and private life separate. They don't usually socialize with colleagues outside working hours.			
f. When you are invited to a person's home for a social occasion, it's usual to arrive ten or fifteen minutes late.			
g. When people give flowers as a present, they give an odd, not an even, number, and without wrapping paper.			

2 What different social customs have you experienced in other countries or other regions of your country? Did any surprise you?

11.1 🔊 **3** A British manager is talking about social customs. He is giving advice about three different countries to a group of trainee international managers. Listen to three extracts from his talk. Tick the topics he talks about in each extract.

Topic	Extract 1	Extract 2	Extract 3
Shaking hands	....	....	....
First/family name	....	....	....
Titles	....	....	....
Business lunches	....	....	....
Punctuality	....	....	....
Humour and jokes	....	....	....
Business cards	....	....	....
Making decisions	....	....	....
Invitations	....	....	....

11.1 🔊 **4** Tick the country you think the manager is describing in each extract. Listen to the extracts again if necessary. Compare answers with a partner.

Extract 1 USA .... Germany .... France ....

Extract 2 Germany .... Spain .... Italy ....

Extract 3 India .... Japan .... China ....

5 Look at the tapescript of Extract 3. Underline three verb forms the manager uses to give advice. Decide which verb forms offer the strongest advice.

Extract 3

So, when you go to this country, you should take plenty of business cards with you. They usually exchange cards at the beginning of a meeting, and they always read your card very carefully. You should do the same with theirs. They might think it rude if you don't. In general, it takes longer for people to make decisions in this country than it does in Britain, so if you want to succeed, you must learn to be patient. And remember that when they say 'Yes', they may mean 'I understand', not 'I agree'. That often causes misunderstandings.

And a final piece of advice – it's not common, but if you receive an invitation to a person's home, you mustn't forget to take off your shoes before going inside, so make sure you're wearing clean socks!

Modal verbs

Modals are special auxiliary verbs which add extra meaning to the main verb.
For example, modals can express advice, necessity, and possibility.

Read the examples. Complete the grammar rules.

should/shouldn't

- You **should** arrive on time. (It's a good idea to arrive on time.)
- You **shouldn't** start discussing business immediately.
  (It's a bad idea to start discussing business immediately.)

● Use ..../*shouldn't* to give advice.

must/mustn't/needn't

- You **must** remember to use people's titles. (It's 100% necessary to remember.)
- You **mustn't** arrive late for meetings. (It's 100% necessary not to arrive late.)
- You **needn't** exchange business cards until the end of the meeting.
  (It's not necessary to exchange cards.)

● Use *must* to express necessity.

● Use .... to express a necessity not to do something.

● Use .... to express no necessity to do something.

may/might

- When they say 'Yes', they **may** mean 'I understand', not I agree. (It's 50% possible.)
- If you make jokes, it **might** make them feel uncomfortable. (It's less than 50% possible.)

● Use *may* and .... to express possibility.

● Use modal verbs without .... before the infinitive.

● To make the negative, add .... to the end of modal verbs.

Do modals have -*s* in the *he/she/it* form?
How do we make questions with modal verbs?

Pocket Book p. 13

Practice **1** Match the modal verbs in A with their meaning in B.

A	B
must	it's a bad idea
mustn't	it's about 50% possible
needn't	it's 100% necessary
should	it's less than 50% possible
shouldn't	it's not necessary
may	it's 100% necessary not to do it
might	it's a good idea

2 Complete the sentences. Use a modal verb which adds the meaning in brackets.

1 If you use a person's first name, you .... offend them. (It's possible.)

2 Decisions take a long time, so you .... learn to be patient.
   (It's necessary.)

3 You .... give an odd number of flowers. (It's advisable.)

4 They .... think it rude if you don't read their business card carefully.
   (It's possible.)

5 You .... wear your outdoor shoes in Japanese homes.
   (It's necessary not to do it.)

6 You .... try to be humorous or make jokes when you don't know
   people very well. (It's not advisable.)

7 You .... give your business card at the beginning of the meeting.
   (It's not necessary.)

3 Work in pairs. You are giving advice to a new company employee. Read the list below. Decide what the new person *must/mustn't/needn't/should/shouldn't* do. Add more ideas.

Example   *You mustn't smoke in the office.*

- introduce yourself
- ask questions
- tell people if you have problems
- arrive punctually every day
- take long breaks
- have a daily meeting with your boss

- find out about the fire regulations
- find out how the phones work
- try to learn people's names
- park in your boss's parking space
- phone your family in Australia from the office

Pronunciation

11.2 🔲 ① Listen to the sentences on the tape. Which word is stressed? Underline it. How does the stress change the meaning of the sentence?

a. You mustn't lose those papers.   b. You mustn't lose those papers.

11.3 🔲 ② Listen to the tape. Underline the stressed word in each sentence.
Example   *You shouldn't do it <u>here</u>.*
    You <u>shouldn't</u> do it here.

1 You might need an umbrella.
2 You should take some cash.
3 You must wear a tie.

4 You shouldn't smoke in here.
5 You mustn't ask for credit.
6 You needn't do it today.

③ Listen again. Repeat the sentences.

④ Work in pairs. Say the sentences in 2 above to your partner. Change the meaning by changing the stress.

---

4 Describe the 'mini-culture' of your company or classroom. Make a list of the things you *must/mustn't/needn't*, or *should/shouldn't* do at work, in class, or at home. Compare your list with a partner.

Example   *You should practise speaking as much as possible.*

5 Work in groups. Prepare some notes for the *Cultural Advice* section of a *Business Traveller's Guide* to your country. Here are some suggestions for topics. Add other topics which are useful to foreigners who are going to visit or work in your country.

Topics
1 Introductions and greetings
2 Punctuality
3 Presents
4 Tipping
5 Queuing
6 Smoking

BUSINESS TRAVELLER'S GUIDE

CHINA

WARICK BOOKS

HUNGARY

Descriptions file. Word building

1 Work in pairs. Match the adjectives in the box to the appropriate descriptions below.

efficient	punctual	honest	polite	sincere
sociable	agreeable	patient	ambitious	flexible

A person who   **Adjective**

1 arrives on time   ....

2 is not rude   ....

3 enjoys the company of other people   ....

4 tells the truth   ....

5 adapts easily to different situations   ....

6 really means what he or she says   ....

7 waits without getting angry   ....

8 works well and doesn't waste time   ....

9 is pleasant and friendly   ....

10 wants to succeed   ....

2 We can make the opposites of some adjectives by adding a prefix, e.g. *un-*, *im-*, *in-*, *dis-*, to the beginning of the adjective. Write the opposites of the adjectives in 1 in the correct column below. Use your dictionary.

un-	*in-*	*im-*	*dis-*
....	*inefficient*	....	....
....	....	....	....
....	....		

3 Describe a 'perfect' English student, work colleague, or personal assistant to your class. Choose adjectives from 1 above.

4 Complete the table below. Use your dictionary to check spelling.

Adjective	Noun
polite	....
flexible	*flexibility*
ambitious	....
punctual	....
efficient	....
honest	....
patient	....

5 Work in pairs. Which of the qualities in 1 are the most important in the jobs below? Which other qualities are necessary?

Example   *A personal assistant must be efficient.*

1 a personal assistant
2 a nurse
3 a politician
4 a shop assistant
5 a teacher
6 a policeman

6 Which qualities do you need in your job?

Cultural differences in body language

1 Discuss these questions.

1 Which nationalities in Europe usually use
   a. a lot of gestures when they speak?
   b. very few gestures when they speak?
2 In conversation, why might a north European move away from, and a south European move closer to, the person they're talking to?
3 Why might north Europeans visiting Mediterranean countries feel uncomfortable at the way people look at them?

Read the text to check your answers.

2 Do you agree with Dr Collett's observations on body language?

Foreign Bodies

Understanding the 'body language' of different nationalities – the way they use gestures, eye-contact, and touching to communicate without words – is an important part of communicating across cultures. In his book *Foreign Bodies*, Oxford University research psychologist, Dr Peter Collett, examines some of the differences among Europeans.

Gesture

Dr Collett suggests that if we compare the way different European nations use gestures, they fall into three groups. In the first group are the Nordic nations – the Swedes, Finns, Norwegians, and Danes – who use gestures very little. The second group includes nations such as the British, Germans, Dutch, Belgians, and Russians. They use some gestures, for example, when they are excited, or want to communicate over long distances, or to insult each other. The third group includes the Italians, Greeks, French, Spanish, and Portuguese. They use gestures a lot, to emphasize what they are saying, and to hold the other person's attention. 'Even when they are silent,' says Dr Collett, 'their hands are often busy sending messages through the medium of manual semaphore.'

Personal space

People's sense of 'personal space' – the distance that separates them from another person – also varies between people of different nationalities. What feels right for one nationality may feel uncomfortable for another. British zoologist, Desmond Morris, has identified three 'personal space' zones in Europe. In countries such as Spain, France, Italy, and Greece, people stand close enough to touch each other easily.

Morris calls this the 'elbow zone'. In East European countries such as Poland, Hungary, and Romania, people stand a little more distant. Morris calls this the 'wrist zone' because they are close enough to touch wrists. In Britain, Holland, Belgium, Germany, and the Scandinavian countries, people prefer to stand further away from each other, and they do not generally touch. This he calls the 'fingertips zone'.

Eye-contact

Another cultural difference between nationalities is the amount of eye-contact between people. In countries where people stand close to each other, in Morris's elbow zone, eye-contact is more frequent and lasts longer. Mediterranean countries, says Dr Collett, are 'high-look' cultures whereas north European countries are 'low-look' cultures. Children who grow up in a low-look culture learn that it is rude to look too long at another person. In a high-look culture, eye-contact, like physical contact and gestures, is a natural way of expressing your feelings and relating to other people. This explains why, for example, north Europeans visiting south European countries may feel uncomfortable at the way people look at them. ■

R E V I E W

3 Work in groups. Compare your answers to the following questions about body language. In your country

1 what gestures do you use to
- call a waiter in a restaurant?
- attract the attention of a friend in a crowd?
- indicate 'Yes' or 'No'?
- show surprise?
- indicate that you don't understand something?
- show anger?

2 how much eye-contact is there between
- people talking to each other?
- strangers passing each other in the street?

3 do people
- stand close enough to touch when they are speaking?
- walk arm-in-arm in public?
- show affection in public (e.g. holding hands, kissing)?

4 Describe any differences you have noticed in the body language of other nationalities. Do you think any of the differences could cause a cultural misunderstanding?

5 Project. Write a short magazine article on body language for visitors to your country.

Social responses

1 How would you respond politely to the following?

1 Sorry I'm late.
2 Thanks for all your help.
3 Have a good weekend.
4 Do you mind if I smoke?

11.4 **2** Listen to some social comments at a party. Tick the most appropriate response.

1 a. Didn't you?
   b. It's Simon. Simon Grant.

2 a. Not at the moment, thanks.
   b. I've had one.

3 a. Yes, that's right.
   b. Yes, I'm from Spain.

4 a. Yes, you are.
   b. Don't worry.

5 a. Yes, you can.
   b. Thank you. That would be very nice.

6 a. Oh, I'm sorry to hear that.
   b. Don't mention it.

7 a. It doesn't matter.
   b. Not at all.

8 a. Thanks, the same to you.
   b. Yes, I hope so.

11.5 **3** Listen to the complete conversations. This time you will hear the most appropriate response. Check your answers.

4 Work in pairs. Look at this picture of guests at a cocktail party. Think of suitable responses to make to their comments and questions.

5 Match the replies to the comments and questions in the picture.

a. Really!
b. Please do.
c. Yes, that's right.
d. It doesn't matter.
e. Thanks. I'll have a whisky.

f. Don't mention it.
g. Well, I'd rather you didn't.
h. Yes, here you are.
i. Never mind. Better luck next time.
j. No, I've been here before.

6 Role-play. You are at Duncan Ross's party at Glencross Castle. Walk around and make small talk with your class colleagues. Practise offering drinks, thanking, apologizing, asking permission, and making appropriate responses.

11.6 **7** Listen to the social comments. Tick the response if it is appropriate.

1 Yes, of course.
2 Thanks. You, too.
3 Yes, here you are.
4 Don't worry.

5 It doesn't matter.
6 I'm sorry to hear that.
7 Yes.
8 Congratulations.

11.7 **8** Listen to the social comments again. This time you will hear an appropriate response. Check your answers.

UNIT 12
Champagne

▼AGENDA

▶ Passives: Present Simple, Past Simple, Present Perfect

▶ Business headlines file. Word families

▷ The champagne market

▷ Thanking for hospitality. Saying goodbye

Language focus ① Who said of champagne, 'In victory you deserve it. In defeat you need it'? When do people in your country drink champagne?

② Work in groups. Read the article about champagne. Answer the questionnaire.

Champagne
What do you know?

CHAMPAGNE OR SPARKLING WINE?

Only wine which is produced in the Champagne region of France can be labelled 'champagne'. In Spain, Australia, the United

States, Germany, Italy, and South Africa sparkling wines are produced in the same way as champagne, using the 'méthode champenoise', but they are not allowed to have the description 'champagne' on their labels.

'LA CHAMPAGNE' AND 'LE CHAMPAGNE'

'La Champagne' is a limited area 140 kilometres north-east of Paris. Vines have been grown in this region of France for more than 2,000 years, but until the 17th century still wine, not sparkling wine, was produced. 'Le champagne' was first made in the 17th century. The experiments of a Benedictine monk, Dom Pérignon, led to the development of the 'méthode champenoise'.

TYPES OF GRAPE

Champagne is made from three types of grape, the black Pinot Noir and Pinot Meunier, and the white Chardonnay grape. These are the only varieties which are permitted in Champagne. Typically, two thirds black grapes and one third white are used to make champagne. 'Blanc de Blancs' is made from white grapes only.

CHAMPAGNE CELLARS

Under the vineyards of Champagne there are 200 kilometres of chalk cellars. They were cut by the Romans and they have been used since Roman times. Their constant 10°C temperature is ideal for producing champagne. This underground chalk extends as far as Britain, where it rises above ground as the White Cliffs of Dover!

VINTAGE AND NON-VINTAGE CHAMPAGNE

Most champagne is non-vintage. Vintage champagne is a champagne which has been produced from the grapes of one particular year. About a hundred days of sun are needed for a vintage year. Non-vintage champagne is made by blending the wine reserves of different years. One of the top champagnes, Krug Réserve, is the result of blending nearly fifty different wine reserves.

CHAMPAGNE
QUESTIONNAIRE

——— 1 ———

Which sparkling wines can put the name 'champagne' on their label?

——— 2 ———

What is the difference between 'la Champagne' and 'le champagne'?

——— 3 ———

Is champagne made from white grapes only?

——— 4 ———

What can you find under the vineyards of the Champagne region in France?

——— 5 ———

Who was Dom Pérignon?

——— 6 ———

What is the difference between vintage and non-vintage champagne?

3 Underline one verb form in each paragraph which is about champagne production. Which tenses are they?

Example *Only wine which is <u>produced</u> in the Champagne region of France can be labelled 'champagne'.*

The Passive

Read the examples. Complete the grammar rules.

Present Simple

- A hundred days of sun **are needed** for a vintage year.
- 'Blanc de Blancs' **is made** from white grapes only.

Past Simple

- The chalk cellars **were cut** by the Romans.
- Champagne **was** first **made** in the 17th century.

Present Perfect Simple

- The chalk cellars **have been used** since Roman times.
- Vintage champagne is a champagne which **has been produced** from the grapes of one particular year.

- To make the passive, use the verb _____ _____ in the correct tense + the past participle of the verb (e.g. *made, produced, grown*).

- Use the _____ when you want to describe actions without describing who does them.

- When we want to say who does the action in a passive sentence, we use the word _____ .

How do we make questions in the passive?

Compare these two sentences.

- *The Romans cut the chalk cellars.*
- *The chalk cellars **were cut** by the Romans.*

 Pocket Book p. 14

Practice ❶ Complete this description of the process of making champagne. Use the Present Simple passive form of the verb in brackets.

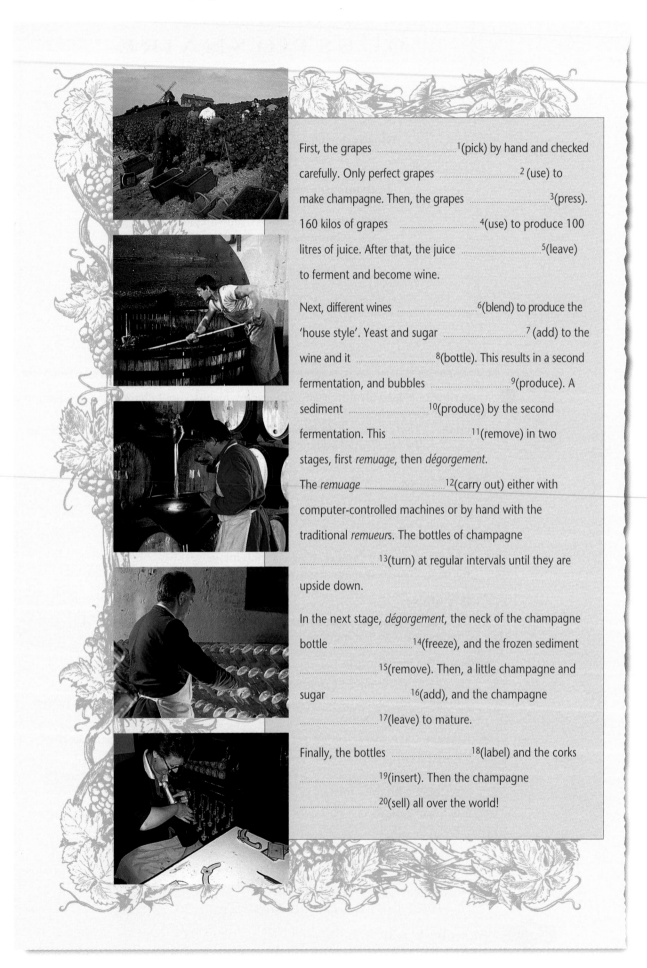

First, the grapes ....[1](pick) by hand and checked carefully. Only perfect grapes ....[2] (use) to make champagne. Then, the grapes ....[3](press). 160 kilos of grapes ....[4](use) to produce 100 litres of juice. After that, the juice ....[5](leave) to ferment and become wine.

Next, different wines ....[6](blend) to produce the 'house style'. Yeast and sugar ....[7] (add) to the wine and it ....[8](bottle). This results in a second fermentation, and bubbles ....[9](produce). A sediment ....[10](produce) by the second fermentation. This ....[11](remove) in two stages, first *remuage*, then *dégorgement*.

The *remuage* ....[12](carry out) either with computer-controlled machines or by hand with the traditional *remueur*s. The bottles of champagne ....[13](turn) at regular intervals until they are upside down.

In the next stage, *dégorgement*, the neck of the champagne bottle ....[14](freeze), and the frozen sediment ....[15](remove). Then, a little champagne and sugar ....[16](add), and the champagne ....[17](leave) to mature.

Finally, the bottles ....[18](label) and the corks ....[19](insert). Then the champagne ....[20](sell) all over the world!

2 Work in pairs. Make questions for these answers from the text.

Examples   *How is vintage champagne made?*
How long has this champagne been left to mature?
When were the chalk cellars cut?

1 How long ....?
They've been grown there for more than 2,000 years.

2 When ....?
It was first made in the 17th century.

3 What ....?
It's made from three types of grape.

4 How ....?
It's made from white grapes only.

5 How long ....?
They've been used since Roman times.

6 How many ....?
About a hundred days of sun are needed.

7 How ....?
It's made by blending the wine reserves of different years.

3 Complete the information about champagne below. Write the passive form of the verbs in brackets.

Champagne facts.
Did you know...?

- Since the beginning of the 20th century, more champagne ....[1](export) to the UK than to any other country, except in 1992. In that year, the highest total ....[2](sold) to Germany.

- In the 17th century, many bottles of champagne ....[3](lose) because the glass was not strong enough to resist the pressure. The problem ....[4](solve) when *verre anglais* ....[5](introduce). This was a much stronger glass which ....[6](produce) in Britain in the 17th century.

- Some champagne houses ....[7](hit) very badly by the Russian Revolution. Ten per cent of total champagne production ....[8](import) by Russian royalty and aristocracy before the Revolution. This market disappeared overnight.

- Champagne ....[9](sell) in eleven different bottle sizes. The smallest is a quarter bottle and it contains twenty centilitres. The biggest, which ....[10](call) a *Nebuchadnezzar*, contains sixteen litres, and is the equivalent of twenty 'normal' 75 centilitre bottles.

4 Work in pairs.

Student A   Read Coffee Factsheet A on p. 110. Ask your partner questions to complete your Factsheet.

Student B   Read Coffee Factsheet B on p. 111. Ask your partner questions to complete your Factsheet.

Examples   **Student A** *How much coffee is exported by Colombia?*
Student B *12,523 bags. Where was the first coffee house opened?*
Student A *In Venice.*

COFFEE FACTSHEET A

PRODUCTION

Coffee is the second most important trading product on the world market. Table 1 shows exportable production of coffee in 1992–3 from major coffee producers. The figures are in millions of 60 kg bags.

TABLE 1	
Major coffee exporters	**Millions of bags**
Brazil	15,950
Colombia	....
Indonesia	....
El Salvador	2,637
Costa Rica	....
Ivory Coast	2,195

CONSUMPTION

.... cups of coffee are drunk in the world every day. On average, seven kilos per capita are bought every year by Europeans. Surprisingly, more coffee is drunk by north Europeans than by south Europeans. Table 2 gives coffee consumption per capita in selected importing countries in 1992. The figures are in kg per capita per annum.

TABLE 2	
Coffee consumers	**kg per capita**
Finland	....
Sweden	11.29
Denmark	....
Austria	9.23
Germany	8.04
France	....
Spain	....
Italy	4.36

HISTORY: SOME KEY FACTS

- Coffee trees were first grown .... years ago.
- Coffee was first drunk by the Arabs.
- It was introduced to Europe by the Venetians in the .... century.
- The first coffee house was opened in Venice in 1615.
- In the 17th century, coffee was served in coffee houses in Austria, France, ..., ..., and ....
- It was taken from Britain to America in the 17th century.

INTERNATIONAL COFFEE AGREEMENT

Since 1962, ... between the coffee exporting and importing countries has been promoted by the *International Coffee Agreement*. As a result of this agreement, the supply and demand for coffee has been balanced and fair prices have been agreed.

PRODUCTION

Coffee is the second most important trading product on the world market. Table 1 shows exportable production of coffee in 1992–3 from major coffee producers. The figures are in millions of 60 kg bags.

TABLE 1

Major coffee exporters	Millions of bags
Brazil	....
Colombia	12,523
Indonesia	7,221
El Salvador	....
Costa Rica	2,624
Ivory Coast	....

CONSUMPTION

1.5 billion cups of coffee are drunk in the world every day. On average, ... kilos per capita are bought every year by Europeans. Surprisingly, more coffee is drunk by .... Europeans than by .... Europeans. Table 2 gives coffee consumption per capita in selected importing countries in 1992. The figures are in kg per capita per annum.

TABLE 2

Coffee consumers	kg per capita
Finland	12.26
Sweden	....
Denmark	11.13
Austria	....
Germany	....
France	5.87
Spain	4.67
Italy	....

HISTORY: SOME KEY FACTS

- Coffee trees were first grown 1,000 years ago.
- Coffee was first drunk by the ....
- It was introduced to Europe by the Venetians in the 17th century.
- The first coffee house was opened in .... in 1615.
- In the 17th century, coffee was served in coffee houses in Austria, France, Germany, Holland, and England.
- It was taken from Britain to America in the .... century.

INTERNATIONAL COFFEE AGREEMENT

Since 1962, co-operation between the coffee exporting and importing countries has been promoted by the *International Coffee Agreement*. As a result of this agreement, the .... and .... for coffee has been balanced and .... have been agreed.

Business headlines file. Word families

1 Work in pairs. Read the headlines. Answer the questions below. Use a dictionary if necessary.

HUGE SLUMP IN CAR SALES

TELECOM COMPANIES COMPETE FOR THE 'BIGGEST CONTRACT OF THE DECADE'

DOMESTIC MARKET HIT BY WORST RECESSION SINCE THE 30s

Boom of the 80s gone forever?

1 Which two words mean 'a period when a country's economy is doing very badly'?
2 Which word means 'a period of ten years'?
3 Which word means the opposite of 'slump' or 'recession'?

MANUFACTURERS CUT PRODUCTION LEVELS

Workers protest at job cuts

4 Is 'cut' used as a verb in both of these sentences?

Signs of recovery in export markets

CONSUMER SPENDING UP ON LAST MONTH

5 Is the news good for exporters?
6 Are people buying less than last month?

2 Complete the table.

Verb	Noun (activity)	Noun (person)
....	competition	a competitor
consume	consumption	a ....
....	exporting	an ....
....	manufacturing	a ....
produce	....	a ....
recover	....	

Pronunciation

12.1 **1** Listen to the tape. Notice the different stress patterns.

· ● ·   · · ● · ·   ● · ·   · · ● ·
a. consumption   b. recovery   c. marketing   d. competition

Australian
domestic
invitation
traveller
financial
occupation
passenger
appreciate

2 Put the words in the box in the correct column.

consumption	recovery	marketing	competition

12.2 **3** Listen and check your answers.

12.2 **4** Listen again. Say each word three times quietly to yourself.

5 Look at the list. Mark the stress pattern on the words.

pronunciation   manager   expedition   corporation
celebration   programmer   exhibition   computer

---

3 Work in pairs. Write two business headlines for a newspaper. Use words from 1 and 2 above. Give your headlines to another pair of students. Read the headlines you receive. Decide what the articles will be about. Write the first sentence of each article.

The champagne market

1 Read these headlines from the early 1990s. What do they mean? What do they tell you about the champagne industry at that time?

CHAMPAGNE'S BUBBLE BURSTS

JOB CUTS TAKE THE FIZZ OUT OF BUBBLY

CHAMPAGNE RECOVERY SOON?

Champagne industry in trouble

12.3 **2** Listen to James Turner interviewing Freddy Price, a wine consultant in champagne's biggest export market, the UK. Complete James's interview notes on the notepad below.

Interview with Freddy Price
10.30 a.m.
Thursday 27 January
Topic – The champagne market

1   1980s – 'boom years'

	Year	No. of bottles
Highest sales		
Highest production level		

2   Decline in market since 80s

Main reasons

1

2

3

3   Price of grapes (per kilo)

	Today	In 1990

4   Market in future

Increase in sales?

Aim of changes

3 Work in groups. Look at the information about either A or B. Use this information to prepare a short presentation. Present your information to the other groups.

A MINERAL WATER

GROUPE DANONE
Europe's largest producer of mineral water

TOTAL MINERAL WATER PRODUCTION IN 1993 – 3.9 BILLION LITRES. LEADING BRAND – EVIAN AND VOLVIC.

SALES BY PRODUCT

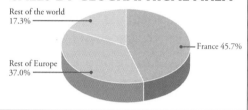

Still water 66.5%
Hotels and leisure 4.4%
Soft drinks 1.6%
Sparkling water 27.5%

OTHER INFORMATION

- Evian – The world's leading exporter of still mineral water. Sales of FF3,130 million in 1993.
- Worldwide exports of Evian up 15% to 481 million litres in 1993. Key markets in the rest of Europe – Switzerland, Germany, and the UK.
- Danone also produces a high energy sports drink – Athlon

THE BEST SELLING MINERAL WATERS - FRANCE, ITALY, SPAIN

France Evian, Volvic, Badoit, Salvetat, Arvie
Italy   Ferrarelle (Market leader, sparkling waters)
Spain   Font Vella, Lanjaron (Very dry weather in southern Spain in 1993 – 10% rise in sales there)

TOTAL SALES 1989 TO 1993
FF million

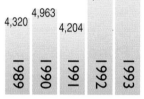

4,320 | 4,963 | 4,204 | 5,979 | 6,353
1989 | 1990 | 1991 | 1992 | 1993

OTHER KEY MARKETS
Japan, Taiwan, Thailand, USA

SALES BY GEOGRAPHICAL AREA

Rest of the world 17.3%
Rest of Europe 37.0%
France 45.7%

B BEER

GROUPE DANONE
Europe's second largest beer producer

TOTAL BEER PRODUCTION IN 1993 – 24.3 MILLION HECTOLITRES

SALES BY PRODUCT

Standard beers 67.3%
Non-alcoholic beers and other 10.1%
Premium and speciality beers 22.6%

OTHER INFORMATION

- Kronenbourg and Kanterbräu – 10.4 million hectolitres produced in 1993. Sales-FF5,459 million in 1993 (down 2% on 1992).
- Sales of premium beers up 6% in 1993. Groupe Danone also produces alcohol-free beer – Tourtel (Sales of alcohol-free beers down in 1992 and 1993.)

THE BEST SELLING BEERS - FRANCE, ITALY, SPAIN

France Kronenbourg, Kanterbräu (Cool summer in France in 1993 – sales down 1.8% on 1992.)
Italy   Peroni
Spain   San Miguel and Mahou

TOTAL SALES 1989 TO 1993
FF million

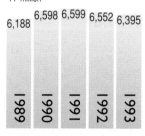

6,188 | 6,598 | 6,599 | 6,552 | 6,395
1989 | 1990 | 1991 | 1992 | 1993

OTHER KEY MARKETS
Greece, Ireland, Switzerland, UK

SALES BY GEOGRAPHICAL AREA

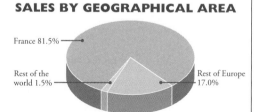

France 81.5%
Rest of the world 1.5%
Rest of Europe 17.0%

4 Project. Collect some facts and figures about one of your country's main exports, e.g. wine, food, or manufactured products. Give a short presentation using your information.

Thanking for hospitality. Saying goodbye

12.4 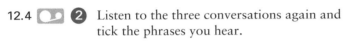 **1** Duncan is saying goodbye to some of the guests who stayed at Glencross Castle after the *Wine and Dine* anniversary celebration. Listen to the three conversations and answer the questions.

Dialogue 1
1 What have Pierre and Anne-Marie invited Duncan to do?
2 Has Duncan accepted?
Dialogue 2
1 What does Monique promise Duncan?
2 When is their next meeting?
Dialogue 3
1 What does Duncan think James should write?
2 Why do you think James asks Duncan about his meeting with Monique?
3 Why do you think James says 'That's the problem'?

12.4 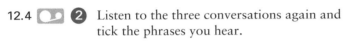 **2** Listen to the three conversations again and tick the phrases you hear.

Thanking for hospitality
Thank you for inviting us.
Thank you very much for your hospitality.
Thank you for everything.
Thanks a lot.

Positive comment
We've had a wonderful time.
I really appreciated it.
It was really enjoyable.
Everything was great.

Responding to thanks

I'm glad you	could come.	See you	on the...	Have a good	trip back.
	enjoyed it.		next week.		flight.
	liked it.		soon.		
	found it interesting.				

Saying goodbye
I really must be going.
We really must leave now.
I must be off.

I look forward to... (*seeing you again*).
I'm looking forward to... (*our next meeting*).

3 Work in pairs. Read the situations below. Practise thanking your partner for hospitality, and make positive comments. Your partner will respond to the thanks. Use phrases from 2 above. Change roles.

1 A colleague has invited you to a restaurant to celebrate your promotion. You have just finished the meal.
2 A supplier has taken you to the theatre to see a play.
3 Some foreign friends have taken you on a sightseeing tour of their city.

4 Read the situations on the left. Match them with an appropriate response on the right.

1 You're at a party. It's late and you want to leave.

a. I really must be going, John. I've got another appointment now.

2 Your business meeting has just finished. You have a train to catch.

b. Thanks for the lift, Sue. I must be off or I'll miss my plane.

3 You've had lunch with a visitor. You have to meet another person in fifteen minutes.

c. Well, I really must leave now. I've got to get to the station.

4 A friend who drove you to the airport is talking to you. You're afraid you'll miss your flight.

d. I must be going. I've got an early start tomorrow.

5 Now walk round and say goodbye to your colleagues. Give your reason for needing to leave now.

REVIEW
UNIT C

▼ **AGENDA**

▷ Grammar   **❶**–**❻**

▷ Social English   **❼**–**⓫**

▷ Vocabulary   **⓬**–**⓭**

This unit reviews all the main language points from units 9–12. Complete the exercises. Check your learning with the Self-check box at the end.

❶ Modals: giving advice

Work in pairs. What advice can you give to a person who

1 needs to learn English as quickly as possible?
2 is travelling to the USA on business for the first time next week?
3 works twelve hours a day, and at weekends, and is always tired?
4 is very disorganized but wants to get a job as a personal assistant?
5 wants to feel healthier and fitter?
6 wants to stop smoking?

❷ Modals: possibility

Work in pairs. Say what you *may* or *might* do

1 next weekend.
2 one evening next week.
3 next summer.
4 next year.

❸ Modals: necessity

Complete these sentences. Use *must*, *mustn't*, or *needn't*.

1 I've got an important meeting tomorrow. I .... be late.

2 I haven't got any money left. I .... go to the bank.

3 We've got plenty of time. We .... hurry.

4 Please check this letter carefully. There .... be any mistakes.

5 These visitors are very important. We .... find a good hotel for them.

6 The restaurant is never full. We .... book in advance.

❹ 1st and 2nd Conditional

Match the two halves of these sentences.

1 If I miss the last flight,
2 If I had more money,
3 If I do more sport,
4 If I had more time,
5 If I spoke better English,
6 If I have the time,
7 If I went jogging every morning,
8 If I pass my exams,

a. I'd learn another language.
b. I'll help you write the report.
c. I could lose weight.
d. I'll apply for the job.
e. I'd buy a bigger house.
f. I'll be healthier.
g. I'd get a promotion.
h. I'll stay at a hotel.

❺ 1st and 2nd Conditional

Write sentences about these future situations. If you think they are possible, write the sentence in the 1st Conditional. If you think they are unlikely, use the 2nd Conditional.

Examples   *If I get a promotion, I'll buy a new car.* (possible)
            If I got a promotion, I'd buy a new house! (unlikely)

1 You get a promotion at work.
2 Your company asks you to work abroad for three years.
3 You win a lot of money.
4 You take six months' holiday from work.
5 You attend an intensive English course in England.
6 You decide to start your own business.
7 You have six children.
8 You win a two-week holiday in China.
9 You learn to fly.
10 You change your career completely.

❻ Passives

Complete the article about the history of chocolate. Write the correct passive form of the verb in brackets.

The Story of Chocolate

Chocolate .... [1] (introduce) to Europe from Mexico by the Spanish in the sixteenth century. In the next century, sugar .... [2] (add), and chocolate .... [3] (make) into a hot drink. As it was very expensive at that time, it .... [4] (drink) only by the rich nobility. The first chocolate factory .... [5] (open) in Switzerland in 1819. Since then, chocolate .... [6] (produce) by factories all over the world, and a huge variety of chocolate products .... [7] (develop). In many countries today, chocolate .... [8] (consume) daily. In Britain, for example, chocolate .... [9] (eat) at least once a week by 75% of the population.

7 Offers and requests

Work in pairs. Make offers and requests and respond to them. Add two more each.
Example   **Student A** *Can you help me with my luggage, please?*
              Student B *Yes, certainly.*

Student A

1 Ask a colleague to lend you a
   dictionary.
2 Offer to help a colleague write a
   letter in English.
3 Offer to phone for a taxi for a
   visitor.
4 Ask ....
5 Offer ....

Student B

1 Ask a friend to give you a lift to the
   station.
2 Ask a colleague to explain a new
   system.
3 Offer to show a visitor round your
   company.
4 Offer ....
5 Ask ....

8 Asking for information

Change these direct questions to indirect questions.
Example   Where's the KLM check-in desk?
              Could you tell me where the KLM check-in desk is?

1 What's the plane fare from Barcelona to Paris?

   Could you tell me .... ?

2 How long does the flight take?

   Do you know .... ?

3 Which airport in Paris does the plane arrive at?

   Can you tell me .... ?

4 When do I need to check in?

   Could you tell me .... ?

5 Can I buy duty-free goods on the plane?

   Do you know .... ?

9 Social responses

Match the comments and questions in A to the responses in B.

A

1 Could I use your dictionary?
2 I didn't get the job I wanted.
3 Have a nice weekend.
4 I'm sorry I'm so late.
5 Do you mind if I smoke?
6 Thanks for all your helpful advice.
7 I've just become a father of twins!
8 Can I get you another drink?

B

a. Don't mention it.
b. Congratulations!
c. Yes, of course.
d. Not at the moment, thanks.
e. I'm sorry to hear that.
f. Thanks. The same to you.
g. It doesn't matter.
h. Well, I'd rather you didn't.

10 Thanking for hospitality

Work in pairs. What would you say in these situations?

1 Your boss has invited you to dinner at his home. You have just finished the meal.
2 A business associate has taken you to a local wine festival.
3 On a business trip, your host has taken you to a restaurant which has local specialities on the menu.
4 Some colleagues at work have given a party to celebrate your promotion.

11 Saying goodbye

Work in pairs. Read the four situations. Explain why you must leave and say goodbye.

Student A

Situation 1
You're talking to a friend on the platform. Your train is coming into the station.

Situation 2
You've just finished a meeting with your boss. You want to leave now to meet a visitor at the airport.

Student B

Situation 3
You've spent a long time helping a colleague. You have an important meeting with a client.

Situation 4
You've had dinner in a restaurant with a customer. It's late and you have to take an early morning flight the next day.

12 Vocabulary

Work in two groups, A and B. Write a vocabulary test to give to the other group. Choose ten of the words below. Write a sentence or phrase to help the other group guess each word.

Example   Word *honesty*
                Clue   *the noun from 'honest'*

motorway	to apologize	headlines	screen	rude	politician	punctuality
slump	to retire	recession	destination	chalk	ambitious	organized
traffic jam	~~honesty~~	speed	boom	keyboard	politeness	

13 Vocabulary test

Give your vocabulary test to the other group. Return the test for marking.
Look at the self-check box below. Tick the areas you need to review.

SELF-CHECK BOX	Yes	No	Pocket Book
● Modals			13
● 1st and 2nd Conditional			11, 12
● Passives			14
● Offers and requests			21
● Asking for information			22
● Social responses			22, 23
● Thanking for hospitality			23
● Saying goodbye			23
● Vocabulary			

Tapescripts

Unit 1

1.1

R=Roberto, J=James, M=Monique

Dialogue 1

J   Roberto! Good to see you again. How are things?
R   Oh, hello, James. Fine, thanks – very busy – lots of work, lots of travelling as always. Can I introduce a good friend of mine, Monique Bresson? Monique, this is James Turner.
M   How do you do.
J   How do you do.

Dialogue 2

J   Are you an importer?
M   No. A translator. I'm here with the Vinexpo translation service. I'm with a group of Italian wine producers who don't speak French.
R   Monique is a genius, James. She speaks five languages fluently.
J   Really? Which ones?
M   Spanish, Italian, and Hungarian, and of course French and English. What do you do?
J   I'm a wine consultant, like Roberto. We both write about wine; I'm a journalist with *Wine and Dine* magazine.

Dialogue 3

J   Actually, I have a job for someone who speaks English and Italian. Are you free later to discuss it?
M   I'm not sure at the moment. I'm afraid I already have several appointments today. Perhaps this evening. How about seven o'clock in the main bar?
J   Fine.

1.2

M=Monique, J=James

J   Ah, Monique.
M   Sorry I'm late.
J   That's OK. A glass of champagne?
M   Thank you. So, what does a wine journalist do?
J   Well, I go to the wine regions and I interview people in the business to get information for my articles. I travel to Italy two or three times a year.
M   Do you enjoy your job?
J   Yes, I really love my work, especially the travelling. I meet so many interesting people.
M   I enjoy travelling, too…
J   Yes, I see from your business card that your translation agency has offices in Paris, London, and Rome. Where do you live?
M   In London. But I often travel in Europe and I come to Paris regularly, usually for work. Sometimes I come to visit my parents. They live near Dijon. So, why do you need a translation agency?
J   Well, to help with interviews for my book about Italian wines.
M   Oh, really? How interesting. We have a lot to discuss!
J   Yes, we do. Do you have time for dinner? The lobster really is excellent.
M   Thank you very much.

1.3

1   Do you travel a lot?
2   How often do you come here?
3   Do you speak French?
4   How often do you go to Italy?
5   Do you work here every year?
6   Who do you meet here?
7   Where does he live?
8   Does James speak Italian?
9   What does Roberto do?
10   Which languages does Monique speak?

1.4

Dialogue 1

T=Tony, M=Monique

T   Excuse me, are you Ms Bresson?
M   Yes, that's right.
T   May I introduce myself? I'm Tony White. How do you do.
M   How do you do, Mr White.

Dialogue 2

J=Jeanne, R=Roberto

J   Roberto! Nice to see you again. How are you?
R   Hello, Jeanne. Fine, thanks. How are you? How's the family?
J   Oh, very well, thank you, Roberto.

Dialogue 3

R=Roberto, L=Luigi, J=James

R   James, I'd like to introduce you to Luigi Bastini. He represents some growers in the Chianti area of Italy here at Vinexpo. Luigi, this is a journalist friend of mine, James Turner.
L   Pleased to meet you, Mr Turner.
J   How do you do. Please call me James.
L   Then you must call me Luigi.

1.5

M=Monique, J=James

J   Monique, I must go now. It was very nice meeting you, and I look forward to seeing you in London next month.
M   I really enjoyed meeting you, too, James. Have a good trip back.
J   Thank you, and the same to you. Bye.
M   Bye. See you soon.

Unit 2

2.1

1   drives
2   visits
3   discusses
4   speaks
5   spends
6   finishes

2.2

P=Peter, I=Interviewer

I   Tell me, Peter, what makes Harrods so famous?
P   Well, it's the biggest department store in the UK – and its Food Hall and Egyptian Hall are very famous. People come to Harrods just to see them.
I   What is special about the Food Hall?
P   It sells many different kinds of food. For example, it has 250 kinds of cheese from all over the world, and more than 180 kinds of bread and patisserie, which 36 pastry chefs prepare every day. Customers also love all the different kinds of chocolate. They buy 100 tons every year.
I   That's amazing! And why is the Egyptian Hall so famous?
P   Well, when people see it they feel they're in another world. It looks like an Egyptian building from 4,000 years ago and it sells beautiful objects. They're not 4,000 years old, of course!
I   Is it true that Harrods produces its own electricity?
P   Yes, it does – 70% – enough for a small town. To light the outside of the building, we use 11,500 light bulbs.

I Really! Tell me, how many customers do you have on an average day, and how much do they spend?

P About 30,000 people come on an average day. But during the sales the number increases to 300,000 customers a day. How much do they spend? Well, on average, customers spend about £1.5 million a day. The record for one day is £9 million.

I £9 million in one day?

P Yes, on the first day of the January sales.

I Harrods says it sells everything, to everybody, everywhere. Is that really true?

P Oh, yes, of course. Absolutely everything…

2.3
R=Receptionist, J=James

R Good morning. Bresson Translation Services.

J Oh, hello. Could I speak to Monique Bresson, please?

R Who's calling, please?

J This is James Turner from *Wine and Dine* magazine.

R Hold the line, please, Mr Turner… I'm sorry. She's in a meeting. Can I take a message?

J Yes. Could you ask her to call me? My number is 0171 331 8579.

R 331 8579. Thank you. I'll give her your message.

J Thank you. Goodbye.

2.4
R=Receptionist, J=James, M=Monique

R Bresson Translation Services.

J Can I speak to Monique Bresson, please?

R Who's calling, please?

J It's James Turner.

R Hold the line, Mr Turner. (*phone rings*) Monique?

M Speaking.

R I have James Turner on line 2 for you…

2.5
R=Receptionist, J=James

R Good afternoon. Bresson Translation Services.

J Good afternoon. This is James Turner again. Is Ms Bresson there, please?

R I'm afraid she's in Paris this afternoon. Can I give her a message?

J Er… yes. Could you tell her that the meeting with Mr Michelmore is on Wednesday at eleven o'clock?

R Could you spell that, please?

J Yes. It's M-I-C-H-E-L-M-O-R-E. And could you ask her to call him? His number is 0171 623 4459.

R Yes, Mr Turner. I'll give her your message.

J Thank you.

Unit 3

3.1
Interview 1
I=Interviewer, M=Massimo Reale

I So, Mr Reale, you come from Italy and you're an engineer. Did you visit the UK on business or for a holiday?

M For both. I attended a two-day international meeting of my company at a hotel in London, then I flew to Scotland with my wife for a holiday.

I How long did you stay there?

M Ten days.

I And how did you spend your time in Scotland?

M Well, we did some sightseeing in Edinburgh. We thought it was a very beautiful city, but we didn't spend all our time there. We rented a car and toured the Scottish Highlands. We also walked in the mountains.

I Did you stay in hotels in Scotland?

M No, we didn't. We stayed in bed and breakfast accommodation in small villages. We met dozens of local people and we found them very friendly, but we didn't always understand them!

I Did you enjoy your holiday?

M Oh, yes, we had a wonderful time. We really needed more time…

3.2
Interview 2
I=Interviewer, L=Dr Lebrun

I So, Doctor Lebrun, you came to London for a medical congress and for a holiday…

L Yes, that's right.

I How many days did you spend in the UK?

L Eight days. The congress lasted three days, and after that I stayed with friends.

I Where did you stay?

L In a hotel for the congress, and then my friends invited me to stay in their London flat.

I Did you go to any museums or art galleries in London?

L Yes, I did. I spent hours in the British Museum and the National Gallery, but I didn't visit the Tate Gallery.

I And what did you do in the evenings?

L My friends and I saw the musical *Cats*, and we ate in some very good restaurants, but I didn't have time to go to the theatre or the opera.

I Did you visit any places outside London?

L Yes. We went to Bath and visited the Roman Baths and took photos of Bath's famous architecture.

3.3

stayed	invited
walked	toured
rented	visited
watched	talked
enjoyed	attended

3.4
R=Receptionist, J=James

R Good afternoon, can I help you?

J Good afternoon. My name's James Turner. I have an appointment with Wayne Brown.

R Oh, yes, Mr Turner. Mr Brown is expecting you. Please take a seat and I'll tell him you're here… Mr Brown, I have Mr Turner in reception for you… OK. Mr Turner, Mr Brown will be with you in a moment.

3.5
W=Wayne, J=James

W Hello, James! Welcome to California! It's good to meet you.

J It's good to be here at last.

W Did you have any problems finding us?

J No. Jack Michelmore gave me directions in London last week. I got a taxi here.

W Good. How was your flight?

J There was a short delay in London, but the flight was fine. Fortunately, I slept on the plane, so I'm not very tired.

W Glad to hear it. You've got a busy programme ahead. Let's discuss it over lunch. I booked a table for one-thirty. Do you like Mexican food?

3.6 🔊

W=Wayne, J=James

W How did your career in the wine business begin?

J Right here, actually. I came to San Francisco when I was a student. That was when I discovered Californian wines.

W When was that?

J Nearly fifteen years ago.

W Did you work in California?

J No. I returned to Europe, and I got a job with a wine merchant. Later, I wrote an article for a wine magazine. That's how it all began! How did you get into the wine business?

W Well, actually, I'm a lawyer. But I grew up in Napa Valley. My uncle owns a winery.

J Really? How big is it?

W Its production is quite small. But the wines are excellent. Anyway, when I finished university my uncle asked me to work for him. I look after his business affairs.

Unit 4

4.1 🔊

a. suitable   b. expensive

4.2 🔊

Example   excitement   b.

1	popular	4	impressive
2	surprising	5	exciting
3	dangerous	6	beautiful

4.3 🔊

1	producer	4	quality
2	consultant	5	translator
3	customer	6	telephone

4.4 🔊

T=Travel consultant

T Good morning, everyone, and thank you for asking me to make this presentation. I'm going to describe three islands in Australia's Great Barrier Reef – they are Hamilton, Heron, and Bedarra. These islands offer a range of accommodation and activities suitable for the different types of people you want to send on this holiday.

First, some general information about Hamilton. It's the largest of the islands, and it has the widest choice of activities. It's the most popular island for young people and has a lively nightlife. It offers more accommodation than the other two islands – there's accommodation for 1,400 people. Prices are high. It has more facilities than the two other islands – lots of restaurants, bars, nightclubs, and shops. It also has the best choice of sporting activities – all the water sports, as well as tennis and golf. So, Hamilton is the biggest and liveliest island, and it offers the most activities.

The second island, Heron, is quieter and more relaxing than Hamilton. It's a national park, and it's a wonderful place for anyone interested in bird-watching. There is accommodation for 250 people, and prices here are lower than on Hamilton. It has only one restaurant and there are no bars or nightclubs. For people who are interested in scuba-diving and snorkelling this island is more exciting than the others because Heron is actually part of the Great Barrier Reef, so when you swim around Heron, you see the thousands of different kinds of tropical fish that make the Great Barrier Reef so famous. So, this island is smaller than Hamilton and is suitable for people who want a quiet place where they can enjoy the wildlife.

The third island, Bedarra, is a lot smaller and more exclusive than the other two islands. People also say it's also the most beautiful. It's an ideal place for people who want to escape noise... and it's even more peaceful than Heron because they don't allow children under 16 years old on Bedarra. There is accommodation for 32 people only, in luxury villas. It's the most expensive island of the three. There are two restaurants which serve very good food and there's a good choice of sporting activities – swimming, wind-surfing, sailing, and tennis. So, to sum up, Bedarra is the smallest, quietest, and most exclusive island of the three.

4.5 🔊

R=Receptionist, J=James

R Hotel Leon d'Oro. Buongiorno.

J Buongiorno. Do you speak English?

R Yes. How can I help you?

J My name is James Turner. Last week I booked a room from the 3rd to the 6th of April... er, you confirmed the reservation by fax.

R Oh, yes, Mr Turner. I remember.

J I'd like to book a single room, for a colleague, for the 4th of April.

R Let me see. Oh, I'm very sorry, Mr Turner, but we're fully booked on the 4th of April, because of Vinitaly, you see.

J Oh, what a pity.

R You could try the other hotels in Verona.

J Yes, I'll do that. Thank you for your help. Goodbye.

R We look forward to seeing you on the 3rd of April, Mr Turner. Goodbye.

4.6 🔊

J Good evening. My name is Turner. I have a reservation.

R Yes, a single room for four nights?

J Yes, that's right.

R Could you fill in this form, please, and sign here? Thank you. Here's your key. Your room is on the first floor. The porter will take your luggage.

J Thank you. Oh, could I have an early morning call, at 6.30?

R Yes, certainly. Do you need anything else?

J No, that's all, thank you.

4.7 🔊

J Could I have my bill, please? Can I pay by credit card or eurocheque?

R Yes, we take both.

J I'll pay by credit card, then.

R That's fine. I hope you enjoyed your stay here.

J Oh, yes, very much. And I'm sure I'll be back here next April, for Vinitaly.

R We'll be delighted to see you again, Mr Turner. Goodbye, and have a good trip back.

J Thank you. Goodbye.

Unit 5

5.1 🔊

M=Martyn, A=Ann

M Hi, Ann. Welcome back! How was your trip to the States?

A Very busy. I had a lot of meetings and, of course, I didn't have much time to see New York.

M What a pity! Actually, I have a trip there myself next week.

A Do you? Then take my advice. Do the *Well-being in the air* programme. It really works.

M Oh, I read about that in a magazine. You say it works?

A Yes. I did the programme on the flight to the States, and when I arrived in New York I didn't have any problems, no jet-lag at all. On the way back I didn't do it and I felt terrible.

M You're joking!

A Not at all. It really made a lot of difference.

M Hmm... So what did you do?

A Well, I didn't drink any alcohol or coffee, and I didn't eat any meat or rich food. I drank a lot of water and fruit juice, and I ate the meals on the *Well-being* menu. They're lighter – they have fish, vegetables, and pasta, for example. And I did some of the exercises in the programme.

M Exercises? On a plane?

A Yes. I didn't do many, of course. There isn't much space on a plane.

M How many passengers did the exercises?

A Not many!

M And how much champagne did they drink?

A A lot! It was more popular than mineral water!

M So, basically it's a choice – mineral water and exercises or champagne and jet-lag?

A That's right. It's a difficult choice!

5.2 🔊

alcohol   information   lemon

5.3 🔊

Example   potato
1   magazine
2   passenger
3   exercise
4   advice
5   problem
6   cigarette
7   vegetable
8   brochure

5.4 🔊

W=Waiter, M=Monique, J=James

W Good evening.

M Good evening. I booked a table for two. The name is Bresson.

W Oh, yes, madam. Your table is over here.

J This is a wonderful surprise, Monique. How did you know it was my birthday?

M Oh, that's a secret. Anyway, I would like to discuss the trip to Hungary with you. You need an interpreter?

J Yes, I do.

M Well, let's order first.

J It's a difficult choice. What do you recommend?

M Well, the fish is usually excellent here. Let's see. I recommend the Dover sole, or if you prefer meat, the Normandy pork.

W Are you ready to order?

M James?

J Yes, I'll have king prawns as starter, and then grilled Dover sole.

M And I'd like smoked salmon and the Normandy pork.

W Certainly, madam. And what would you like to drink?

M You choose.

J OK. A bottle of Sancerre, please.

5.5 🔊

M This wine is very good, isn't it? Do have some more, James.

J Yes, it's very good, and the fish is delicious.

M Good. I'm pleased you like it. Now, how about a dessert?

J I'm sure they're all wonderful, Monique. Thank you, but I couldn't eat any more.

M Are you sure? Would you like some coffee, then?

J Yes. That would be very nice.

M Now, about the trip to Hungary...

5.6 🔊

J Thank you for a lovely evening, Monique. I really enjoyed it.

M Don't mention it. I enjoyed it very much, too, James.

J Now. When's *your* birthday?

Unit 6

6.1 🔊

I=Interviewer, O=Olivia Lonro

I Could you tell me more about your first job, with Hotel Marketing Concepts?

O Yes, certainly. I was a marketing consultant, responsible for marketing ten UK hotels. They were all luxury hotels, in the leisure sector, all of a very high standard.

I Which markets were you responsible for?

O For Europe and Japan.

I I see from your CV that you speak Japanese. Have you ever been to Japan?

O Yes, I have. I spent a month in Japan in 1993. I met all the key people in the tourist industry – the big tour operators and the tourist organizations. As I speak Japanese, I had a very big advantage...

I Yes, of course. Have you had any contact with Japan in your present job?

O Yes, I've had a lot. Cruises have become very popular with the Japanese, both for holidays and for business conferences. In fact, the market for all types of luxury holidays for the Japanese has increased a lot recently.

I Really? I'm interested to hear more about that, but first, tell me, have you ever travelled on a luxury train, the Orient Express, for example?

O No, I haven't. But I've travelled on the Glacier Express through Switzerland, and I travelled across China by train about eight years ago. I love train travel. That's why I'm very interested in this job...

6.2 🔊

a.   I don't think I have.
b.   Have you heard this before?
a.   He hasn't arrived.
b.   Robert has forgotten.

6.3 🔊

1   I think he has.
2   Have you seen him today?
3   The invoice has arrived.
4   She hasn't been here today.
5   I haven't read the instructions.
6   Yes, I have.
7   Many people have said that.
8   Inflation has gone down this year.

6.4 🔊

C=Careers officer

C What makes a good interview? First, good preparation before the interview. Prepare yourself by following three simple guidelines. Guideline number one is – find out as much as possible about the company. For example, you can get a lot of useful information from the company's brochures, annual reports, catalogues, that sort of thing. Two, find out if the interview is with one person or with a group of people, and what their jobs are. It's very useful to know something about the interviewers before you meet them. And three, make a checklist of the questions you want to ask at the interview. Remember an interview is a two-way process. The company finds out as much as possible about you, and you find out as much as possible about the company.

So, that's what you need to do before the interview. Now, the interview itself. There are seven more guidelines to remember here. Guideline number four, dress smartly. A suit or something formal is best. Five, arrive in good time. Arriving late for the interview is the worst thing you can do. Rule number six, create a good first impression. Remember, first impressions are very important. Start the interview with a smile, a firm handshake, and a friendly manner.

Guideline number seven? Try to stay positive and relaxed during the interview. I know that's difficult. People don't usually feel relaxed during an interview, but remember, your body language gives the interviewer a lot of information about you. You want that information to be positive, not negative. Number eight – don't give only 'Yes' or 'No' answers. Talk freely about yourself, give reasons for your opinions, and explain why you're interested in the job. Nine – ask questions. Remember the check-list of questions you prepared before the interview. Show you're interested! Finally, guideline number ten: learn from the interview. Analyse your performance afterwards and think how you can improve the next time!

6.5 📼

R=Receptionist, M=Monique, D=Duncan
R Monique, I have a Mr Duncan Ross on the line.
M Oh, yes, put him through… Hello, Mr Ross. Thank you for your letter. I'd be very interested to meet you and discuss the new project…
D That's very good news. Oh, please call me Duncan, by the way. When would be convenient for you?
M Let me see… I'm rather busy this week… Is next week possible for you? I'm free on Tuesday… or Friday, if you prefer?
D No, Tuesday suits me fine. Shall we say lunch on Tuesday, then?
M Yes, that's fine. What time would suit you?
D How about one thirty at Claret's restaurant?
M Oh, that'll be very nice.
D Good. Well, I look forward to meeting you again, Monique.
M It'll be very nice to see you again, too, Duncan. Goodbye.

6.6 📼

M=Monique, D=Duncan
M Hello. Is that Duncan Ross?
D Yes, speaking.
M Oh, hello, Duncan. It's Monique Bresson here. I'm very sorry. I'm afraid I can't manage our meeting on Tuesday. I have to go to Rome on that day. Could we arrange another time?
D Oh, what a pity. But yes, of course. When are you free?
M Is Thursday the 17th possible for you?
D No, I'm afraid I've got another appointment then. What about Friday the 18th?
M Yes, I can make it on Friday.
D Very good. So, the same time and place? One thirty, at Claret's?
M Yes. Thank you, Duncan. And I do apologize.
D Don't mention it. It's no problem at all. Have a good trip to Rome. See you on Friday…

Unit 7

7.1 📼

P=Radio presenter, S=Susan Hill
P Hello, and welcome to another programme in our series, *Working abroad*. Our guest this evening is an English person who lives and works in Italy. Her name is Susan Hill… Susan, welcome to the programme. You live in one of Italy's most famous cities – Florence. How long have you been living there?
S I've been living in Florence since 1982. But when I went there in 1982, I planned to stay for only six months.
P Why did you change your mind?
S Well, I'm a designer. I design leather goods, mainly shoes and handbags. Soon after I arrived in Florence, I got a job with one of Italy's top fashion houses, Ferragamo – so I decided to stay!
P How lucky! Do you still work for Ferragamo?
S No. I've been a freelance designer for quite a long time now, since 1988, in fact.
P So does that mean you design for several different companies now?
S Yes, that's right. Since I went freelance, I've designed a lot of fashion items for Italian companies. And in the last four years, I've also been designing for the British company, Burberrys.
P What have you been designing for them?
S Mostly handbags and small leather goods.
P Has the fashion industry in Italy changed since 1982?
S Oh, yes. It's become a lot more competitive – because the quality of products from other countries has improved a lot. But Italian quality and design is still world-famous.
P And do you ever think of returning to live in England?
S No, not really. I've made a lot of important contacts in the fashion industry, and for a freelance designer, working in Italy is a lot easier, and more interesting! And, of course, it's not only the work – I really love the sun and the lifestyle!
P Have you been to England this year?
S No. I haven't had time. I've been travelling a lot recently. I've just visited a factory in Modena, for example, and I've been to Germany a few times since Christmas.
P And have you had any free time in your busy work schedule?
S Well, unfortunately, I've had very little free time this year, but I've been visiting friends more in the last few months. I feel that I've been working too much this year, so I've been trying to relax more…
P Well, thank you for talking to us, Susan.
S It was a pleasure.

7.2 📼

a. I've lived here for fifteen years.
   Have you?

b. I've lived here for fifteen years.
   Have you?

a. I work in Helsinki.
   Really?

b. I work in Helsinki.
   Really?

7.3 📼

1 I work in the city centre.
   Do you?
2 I didn't have time to finish yesterday.
   Didn't you?
3 I've been working very hard this week.
   Have you?
4 I don't like jazz.
   Don't you?

5 We went to a restaurant for lunch.
    Did you?
6 I've never visited Rome.
    Haven't you?

7.4

1 I often travel on business.
    Do you?
2 I didn't speak to him last week.
    Didn't you?
3 I've been living here for ages.
    Have you?
4 I don't eat meat.
    Don't you?
5 We visited all the major cities last year.
    Did you?
6 I've never been to the opera.
    Haven't you?

7.5

J=James, D=Duncan

J Sorry I'm late, Duncan. The traffic was terrible…
D Oh, don't apologize. I'm glad you could find time for a meeting.
J OK, so you want to discuss how we celebrate the tenth anniversary of *Wine and Dine*, right?
D Yes. First, what do you think about having the celebration at my castle in Scotland, instead of at a London hotel?
J Well, in my opinion, Scotland is too far for people to travel.
D Yes, I agree. So I thought of chartering a plane from London. We could include travel to Scotland in the invitation. What's your opinion of that?
J I think that's a really great idea!
D Good. Second, how do you feel about celebrating the publication of your new book on Italian wines at the same time?
J That's a wonderful idea, Duncan! I certainly agree with that.
D I thought you'd like that idea! Now, we need to decide on the programme. What do you think about this idea…

7.6

D=Duncan, J=James

D OK, James. Then I suggest you give a talk on Italian wines.
J How about having a tasting of Italian wines?
D Yes, let's do that. Right, that's a very full programme on the first day. Do you have any suggestions for the second day?
J Why don't we make the second day more relaxing? Give people an opportunity to socialize, to get to know each other better. Why not start the day with a champagne breakfast?
D Yes, and we could follow that with a treasure hunt in the garden, with a bottle of something very special as the treasure?
J Hmm, I'm not sure about that. What if it rains?
D Don't worry, James. We have wonderful summers in Scotland. And then people can choose – there's tennis, swimming, golf.
J In fact everything for a great weekend of celebration!
D That's right. And we finish with a big party in the evening. Well, James, I think we've agreed on everything. All we need now is to check the guest list, and make sure we haven't forgotten anyone…

Unit 8

8.1

P=Press Officer, N=Nick Lander, K=Kiki Johns

P Good evening. My name is Julie Waite. Welcome to the Pacific Hotel and to this press briefing. I know you want more information about tomorrow's Grand Opening, so let's begin with your questions.
N Could you give us more details about the President's arrival?
P Yes. The President is arriving by helicopter at 10 a.m.
N Right. And where is he making the opening speech?
P In the Conference Room on the first floor. But we're not having the champagne reception there, that's taking place in the garden, from eleven to eleven thirty.
K What exactly is the Oriental menu presentation at 14.00?
P Two of our chefs are presenting our special 'Oriental menu' – that's the menu we serve in the Oriental Restaurant.
N Is the President taking a balloon flight in the afternoon?
P No, he isn't. The balloon flights are for journalists and TV cameramen. If you'd like to take one of the flights, please give me your name after this briefing.
N/K/other journalists Oh, yes. What a great idea!
P Any more questions about tomorrow's programme? No? Then let's go on to the next part of our briefing…

8.2

N=Nick Lander, K=Kiki Johns

N What a wonderful idea! Are you going to take a balloon flight?
K Yes, of course. Think of the fantastic photos we can get from the air, the Roof Garden, the swimming pool.
N Yes. And I'm going to take photos of the President's arrival by helicopter, on the hotel roof.
K Good idea. What are you going to write about?
N Oh, everything. It's such a marvellous hotel. I'm going to write a lot about the business facilities. They're the best I've ever seen – the latest technology, the fastest communication links. That's very important for the readers of my magazine – they're all business people, you see. What about you?
K Well, I'm definitely not going to describe the hotel's business facilities! My readers come to a hotel like this for a holiday, not for work! No, I'm going to write about the leisure facilities, the Roof Garden, and the oriental cuisine…

8.3

a. Who do I speak to?   b. Can I speak to John?

8.4

Example   You can speak to him tomorrow.   b.
1 We're going to see him tomorrow.
2 Did you listen to the news this morning?
3 Paolo is a man you can talk to.
4 You can write to me at my office.
5 You can talk to Paolo.
6 What address do I write to?

8.5

Air France flight 962 to Marseilles is now ready for boarding. Please proceed to Gate number 11. Gate 11 for flight AF 962 to Marseilles.

Passengers travelling to Dusseldorf on Lufthansa flight

4037 are requested to proceed to Gate number 28. Flight LH 4037, now boarding at Gate number 28.

Iberia Airways regret to announce the delay of flight IB 3915 to Malaga. This flight is now scheduled to leave at 11.50.

Final call for Alitalia flight 287 to Venice. Please go immediately to Gate 15.

This is the final call for Olympic Airways flight 259 to Athens. This flight is now closing at Gate 19.

8.6

1 Your attention, please. Would Mrs van Slooten, travelling to Amsterdam, please contact the KLM information desk.

2 We are now ready to board. Would passengers in seat rows 17 to 22 board first. Please have your boarding cards ready.

3 Your attention, please. Will the person who left a black briefcase in the transfer security area please return there to collect it immediately.

4 May I have your attention, please. This is a special announcement. Will Mr Balmain, the last remaining passenger for flight SR 836 to Geneva, please go immediately to Gate 5, where his aircraft is waiting to depart.

5 May I have your attention, please. This is a security announcement. Passengers are reminded not to leave their bags unattended at any time.

8.7

1 Please fasten your seat-belts.
2 Smoking is not allowed in rows 1 to 6 and 10 to 22, and in the toilets.
3 Please make sure your seat is in the upright position for take-off.
4 We will shortly be serving drinks and a light meal.
5 Non-EU passengers are required to fill in a landing card.
6 Please remain seated until the aircraft has come to a complete standstill.

8.8

D=Duncan Ross, M=Monique Bresson
D Hello. Duncan Ross.
M Hello, Duncan. It's Monique Bresson. My secretary said you called.
D Yes. Thank you for calling back. I wanted to make sure you've received the invitation.
M Yes, I have. Thank you. I'd be delighted to accept.
D Good. Er... Monique, some friends of mine are going to stay at Glencross for a few days after the celebration, and I'd like to invite you to stay, too. Would you join us for four or five days?
M Oh, I'd love to, Duncan, but I'm afraid I can't. I've already arranged to go to Brussels on the 18th...
D Well, would you like to stay until the 17th? I'm sure you need a break from your busy schedule. You work too much, Monique!
M You're right. Thank you, Duncan, I'd love to stay until the 17th.

8.9

J=James Turner, D=Duncan Ross
J Hello.
D Hello, James, it's Duncan. How's everything? I hope you're ready for the big event at Glencross!
J Not yet, but there's still time.
D James, some friends are going to stay at Glencross for a few days after the celebration. How about joining us?

J Thanks a lot, Duncan, I'd love to, but I'm going to be very busy during that week.
D That's a pity. Monique Bresson is going to stay and I know you enjoy her company.
J Is she really? Then let me think about it, Duncan perhaps I can manage to change a few appointments...

Unit 9

9.1
a. printer   b. Sweden

9.2
Example   will   *a.*
1 still   5 please
2 three   6 key
3 trip   7 visit
4 speed   8 grilled

9.3

C=Clive Girling, Product Marketing Manager for Apple Computer UK

C The first thing I'd like to say about the Newton MessagePad is that it's as easy to use as pencil and paper. It doesn't have a keyboard like a computer, you simply write on the screen with a pen. The Newton reads your handwriting and changes it into typed text. And it recognizes pictures as well, so you can draw maps and diagrams, for example.
Second, the Newton MessagePad is very personal. It learns about you – your daily programme, your meetings, your friends. It helps you to organize your life, like a personal assistant. For example, if you write on the MessagePad 'lunch with John, Tuesday', it'll find the information about 'John' in the Name file. Then it'll write the lunch appointment in the Date Book for the next Tuesday, at the time you usually have lunch.
Third, the Newton helps you to communicate. For example, if you want to phone John about the lunch appointment, it'll dial his phone number for you. If you prefer to send John a fax, with a map of the restaurant, then you can do that too, using a standard telephone line, or you can connect your Newton to a printer and send John a printed letter. Your Newton can also communicate with other computers by electronic mail.
So, I hope that gives you some idea of the ways you can communicate with other people using the Newton. But there are hundreds of other things you can do with your Newton, using the different software applications on the market. And of course, a company can produce its own software and use the Newton to do particular jobs in that company. I think the Newton MessagePad really is the beginning of a new age in telecommunications and personal computing.

9.4

D=Duncan Ross, C=Carol, Duncan's secretary
D (*phone*) Oh, Carol, can you come into my office? It's about my trip to France.
C Yes, of course. (*Carol arrives*) So, you have meetings in Paris on Monday and Tuesday.
D Yes. I'll be in Scotland at Glencross the week before, so could you book me a flight from Edinburgh to Paris on Sunday afternoon or evening if possible?
C Right. Shall I book a hotel in Paris for those three nights?

D Yes, please. Then on Wednesday I want to travel to Bordeaux, either by train or plane.

C Would you like me to get some information on both?

D Thank you. I'd appreciate that. I need to be in Bordeaux by about 1 p.m. I think the TGV is probably best. Would you mind checking arrival times of the TGV and the plane?

C No, of course not.

D Right, thanks very much, Carol. That's all for the moment. I'm not sure about the trip back yet, but we can arrange that later.

9.5 🔊

D (phone) Carol, I'd like to give you the other details about my trip to France.

C Yes, fine. I'll come in.

D Right, I need to be back in London on the Friday evening. Do you think you could check the times of direct flights from Bordeaux?

C Yes, certainly. What about accommodation? Do you want me to book a hotel in Bordeaux?

D Thanks, but that won't be necessary. I'm going to stay with some friends. They've got a little château and some vineyards, and they produce some very good wine.

C Mm, it sounds a lot more enjoyable than a hotel.

D Yes, I think it will be.

Unit 10

10.1 🔊

P=Presenter of radio programme, C1/C2/C3/C4=Callers to radio phone-in programme

P Good morning, and welcome to *Viewpoint*. Today's programme is about the problem of traffic congestion in our cities and on our roads. In the next twenty years the number of cars will double. Already traffic jams cost industry billions of dollars a year and there are 50,000 road deaths a year in Europe. What do you want the government to do about this problem? We're waiting for your calls. Call us now. Yes, we have our first caller on the line...

C1 Hello. Well, I'd like the government to spend money on improving public transport in cities. If we had a really good public transport system, we wouldn't need to use our own cars so much. We could park outside the city centre, and then use public transport inside the city. If we did that, we could all move around a lot more quickly.

P Right, so you think the answer is a better public transport system. Thank you, and let's hear from our second caller...

C2 Yes, well, I agree with the last caller, but good public transport costs a lot of money. I think we could make some of that money if we charged people for driving in cities. Make car drivers pay a fee! If motorists had to pay to drive in city centres, they would use their cars a lot less. And that would also mean fewer traffic jams.

P A good point, yes. Make drivers pay a fee. What do you think? Call us now. Ah, we have our third caller on the line... Hello?

C3 Well, I'm against building more and more motorways. This government thinks that if we had more motorways, we wouldn't have traffic jams on our roads, but that's just not true. More motorways mean more cars. If I were the Transport Minister, I would stop building motorways and spend the money on railways.

P Yes, I'm sure other listeners would agree with you on that. What does our fourth caller think? Hello?

C4 Good morning. Well, I would ban cars completely from city centres. If we didn't have all those cars, we wouldn't have all that pollution and noise. We need to think more about the people who live and work in cities, and their health. We want cities for people, not cities for cars.

P Right, thank you to those listeners. And now to discuss your ideas we have on our panel...

10.2 🔊

a. I'd do more sport if I had enough time.
b. If I earned more money, I'd buy a new car.

10.3 🔊

1 If I had a car, I'd drive it to work.
2 If I lived in the city, I'd travel by bike.
3 I'd take more exercise if I were you.
4 If they banned all cars, the air would be cleaner.
5 If the buses were quicker, more people would use them.
6 Would you take the train if you could?

10.4 🔊

R=Reservations clerk, BA Executive Club, C=Carol, Duncan Ross's secretary,

R British Airways reservations. How can I help you?

C I'd like some information about flights from Edinburgh to Paris, on a Sunday afternoon, please.

R Certainly. Let me check. OK. There's one flight at 14.45, and two later flights at 16.00 and 18.00 hours. They all involve a transfer at Heathrow.

C What time does the first flight arrive?

R At 18.45.

C Could you repeat that, please?

R Certainly. 18.45.

C And when do the later flights arrive?

R The 16.00 gets in at 20.50, and the 18.00 at 23.05.

C Right, I've got that. Could you tell me the times of flights from Bordeaux to London, travelling on a Friday?

R I'll look that up. Right, there's just one British Airways flight daily, leaving at 14.40 and arriving at Gatwick at 15.10.

C Do you know if Air France flies from Bordeaux to London?

R I'm afraid I don't have any information about Air France flights. I can give you their telephone number.

C No, don't worry, I think the 14.40 flight will be fine. Thank you for the information. I'll get back to you later to book the flights.

10.5 🔊

F = Clerk at French Railways London office, C = Carol

F Good afternoon, French Railways.

C Good afternoon. I'd like to know the times of trains from Paris to Bordeaux.

F Can you tell me when you want to travel?

C Yes, on a Wednesday, arriving in Bordeaux by about 1 p.m.

F There's a TGV which arrives in Bordeaux at exactly 1 p.m.

C Oh, that's lucky. Could you tell me when it leaves?

F Yes, it leaves at 10 a.m.

C So the journey takes three hours?

F Yes, that's right.

C And do you know which station it leaves from?

F Yes, from Paris Montparnasse.

C Thank you. Oh, just one more question. Do I need to make a reservation?

F   Yes, it's advisable.
C   OK. I'll check with my boss, then phone you back. Thank you for your help.
F   You're welcome.

Unit 11

11.1

M=British manager giving a talk
Extract 1
M   So, it's important to know about the differences in culture between your country and the country you're visiting or working in. If you don't know the social customs, you may make mistakes and offend people…
Handshaking is one example. In this country they shake hands much more than we do in the UK – every day, in fact, so you mustn't forget to do that. Another difference is that at work they use first names much less than we do in Britain, so call people by their family names. Food and wine are very important in this country, and at a business lunch you shouldn't start discussing business immediately. That might seem like bad manners. If you receive an invitation to a person's home, take good chocolates, flowers, or a good bottle of cognac. You shouldn't take wine because they drink that every day – it's too ordinary…

Extract 2
M   Yes, for example in Britain, we often arrive five or ten minutes late for a meeting but in this country you should arrive on time, because people are normally very punctual in work situations. They usually arrive at the arranged time or earlier.
Family names, not first names, are more common at work and people use titles – Doctor and Professor, and so on. So you must remember to do the same. Your colleague will tell you if he or she wants you to use their first name.
Another difference is that you shouldn't try to be humorous or make jokes with people you don't know very well, because it might make them feel uncomfortable. Business meetings are usually serious. It's normal to exchange business cards at a first meeting, but you needn't do this until the end of the meeting. For social invitations, flowers or chocolates are suitable gifts. And you should give an odd number of flowers, say, eleven or thirteen, not twelve, and present them without the wrapping paper…

Extract 3
M   So, when you go to this country, you should take plenty of business cards with you. They usually exchange cards at the beginning of a meeting, and they always read your card very carefully. You should do the same with theirs. They might think it rude if you don't.
In general, it takes longer to make decisions in this country than it does in Britain, so if you want to succeed, you must learn to be patient. And remember that when they say 'Yes', they may mean 'I understand', not 'I agree'. That often causes misunderstandings.
And a final piece of advice – it's not common, but if you receive an invitation to a person's home, you mustn't forget to take off your shoes before going inside, so make sure you're wearing clean socks!

11.2

a.   You mustn't lose those papers.
b.   You mustn't lose those papers.

11.3

Example   You shouldn't do it here.
            You shouldn't do it here.
1   You might need an umbrella.
2   You should take some cash.
3   You must wear a tie.
4   You shouldn't smoke in here.
5   You mustn't ask for credit.
6   You needn't do it today.

11.4

1   I'm sorry. I didn't catch your name.
2   How about a drink?
3   You're from Spain, aren't you?
4   Sorry I'm late.
5   Can I get you something to eat?
6   We've got a lot of problems at the moment.
7   Thanks very much for your help.
8   Have a good weekend.

11.5

1   I'm sorry. I didn't catch your name.
    It's Simon. Simon Grant.
2   How about a drink?
    Not at the moment, thanks.
3   You're from Spain, aren't you?
    Yes, that's right.
4   Sorry I'm late.
    Don't worry.
5   Can I get you something to eat?
    Thank you. That would be very nice.
6   We've got a lot of problems at the moment.
    Oh, I'm sorry to hear that.
7   Thanks very much for your help.
    Not at all.
8   Have a good weekend.
    Thanks, the same to you.

11.6

1   May I use your phone?
2   Have a good holiday.
3   Could I ask you something?
4   I'm sorry, I've got the wrong number.
5   Thanks for the lovely flowers.
6   Someone stole my car last night.
7   Do you mind if I join you?
8   I'm getting married tomorrow.

11.7

1   May I use your phone?
    Yes, of course.
2   Have a good holiday.
    Thanks. You, too.
3   Could I ask you something?
    Yes, go ahead.
4   I'm sorry, I've got the wrong number.
    Don't worry.
5   Thanks for the lovely flowers.
    Don't mention it.
6   Someone stole my car last night.
    I'm sorry to hear that.
7   Do you mind if I join you?
    Not at all.
8   I'm getting married tomorrow.
    Congratulations.

Unit 12

12.1

a.   consumption
b.   recovery

c. marketing
d. competition

12.2
Australian
domestic
invitation
traveller
financial
occupation
passenger
appreciate

12.3

J=James Turner, F=Freddy Price

J Mr Price, what changes have you seen in the champagne market in the last ten to fifteen years?

F Well, the biggest change has been the decrease in sales since the great 'boom' years of the 1980s, when champagne production and sales reached record levels.

J Which was the best year?

F Well, the record was in 1989, when 249 million bottles of champagne were sold. The highest production level was reached in 1990, with a total of 293 million bottles. Of course, since those boom years sales have fallen.

J Has the market been badly hit by the recession?

F Oh, certainly. The economic problems in champagne's export markets – that's Europe, the United States, Japan, and of course the domestic market in France – the economic problems have certainly been one reason for the decrease in champagne sales.

J And the other reasons?

F Another important factor has been price. In the early 90s, champagne was very over-priced, so many people stopped buying it. Instead they bought sparkling wines from other countries – in particular from Australia, California, and Spain. And then, there was another problem for champagne in the early nineties.

J What was that?

F There was a lot of rather bad champagne on the market. This meant the popularity of good sparkling wines increased even more. People were surprised by their quality and, of course, they were a lot cheaper than champagne.

J Have champagne producers been forced to reduce their prices because of this competition?

F Well, champagne prices have come down since the early 90s, but I think this is more because of the reduction in the price of grapes than because of the competition from sparkling wines. Today the price of grapes is around 20 French francs a kilo – a lot more realistic than the 1990 price of about 36 francs a kilo.

J Do you think the champagne market will recover in the future?

F Oh, I'm sure it will. When the economic situation improves, I believe the market will recover. Recently some important changes have been introduced. The aim is to make sure the producers meet very high standards and produce the best quality. I think these changes will produce very good results.

J So, that's good news for the consumers of those 200 million bottles a year?

F Yes, certainly. In fact, good news for all of us.

12.4

P=Pierre, D=Duncan, A=Anne-Marie, M=Monique, J=James

Dialogue 1

P Duncan, we really must leave now or we'll miss our plane back to Bordeaux. Thank you for inviting us, we've had a wonderful time.

D I'm glad you enjoyed it, Pierre. And thank you for inviting me to stay with you. I'm really looking forward to it.

A And so are we. Goodbye, Duncan. See you next week in Bordeaux.

D Goodbye, Anne-Marie, Pierre. Have a good flight.

Dialogue 2

M Duncan, thank you very much for your hospitality. I really appreciated it.

D Well, I'm very pleased you agreed to stay a few more days. You must come and stay whenever you like, Monique.

M Thank you, I promise I will. So, goodbye, Duncan. See you in London on the 22nd.

D Yes, I'll ring you next week to fix the time. Goodbye, Monique.

Dialogue 3

D Well, James, thanks for all your help organizing the *Wine and Dine* celebration, and congratulations – everybody was very impressed by your book! I think you should write another one!

J Yes, I'll think about it. Er, Duncan, you're meeting Monique in London on the 22nd?

D Yes. To discuss the French edition of *Wine and Dine*. Monique has agreed to do all the translation work.

J Oh, good, I thought… well…

D Don't worry, James, it's strictly business. Although I must say Monique's a very attractive and interesting person!

J Yes, I know, that's the problem. Well, I must be off. I'm driving Monique to the airport. Thanks a lot, Duncan. Everything was great.

D Bye, James, and don't forget to think about that second book, not just your social life! Bye, James. (*shouts*) Bye, Monique.

Answer key

Unit 1

Language focus   p. 2

1   Vinexpo is an important international wine trade fair which takes place in Bordeaux every two years. People discuss the wine business. They taste new wines and arrange contracts and business deals.

2   (Possible answers)
Roberto is a wine consultant. He works in Florence.
His telephone number is 055 53 75 866.
Bresson Translation Services has offices in London, Paris, and Rome.
James is a wine journalist.
He works in London.
His office is in Honeywell Street.

3   1   No, he doesn't.
2   How do you do. How do you do.
3   She is with the Vinexpo translation service, to translate for a group of Italian wine producers.
4   What do you do?
5   Because he has a job for her.
6   At 7 o'clock that evening.

4   1   interviews people
2   two or three times a year
3   London

- Use the Present Simple to talk about long-term situations and routine activities.
- To make the question, use *do* + *I/you/we/they* + infinitive.
- The positive form always ends in -*s*.
- To make the negative, use *does* + *not* + infinitive.
- To make the question, use *does* + *he/she/it* + infinitive.

Practice   p. 3

1   1   writes
2   doesn't import
3   meet
4   doesn't live
5   don't speak
6   travels

2   1   Who?
2   When?
3   What?
4   Where?
5   Which?

3   1   Where do they live?
2   How often does he go there?
3   Where do they meet?
4   When does she visit them?
5   Who do they meet at Vinexpo?
6   What does he write about?

Pronunciation   p. 4

1   1 a.   2 b.   3 a.   4 b.   5 a.
6 b.   7 b.   8 a.   9 b.   10 b.

- In questions that begin with question words, the voice goes down at the end.

4   1   Does Monique speak Italian? Yes, she does.
2   Where does she work? In London, Paris, and Rome.
3   Do James and Roberto write about wine? Yes, they do.
4   Does James work for *Wine and Dine*? Yes, he does.
5   Does Roberto know Monique? Yes, he does.
6   Does James live in Italy? No, he doesn't.
7   Does he love his work? Yes, he does.
8   Does James go to France and Italy? Yes. Two or three times a year.
9   Where do Monique's parents live? Near Dijon.
10   Does she travel to Paris? Yes, she does.

5

5   Group A (Possible questions)
Which magazine is the letter from?
What does James do?
Does he often travel in Europe?
Who does he interview?
What are his hobbies/interests?
Which sports does he play?
Does he enjoy English cooking?
Group B (Possible questions)
Why is Monique at Vinexpo?
Which stand is she on?
Does she live in Paris?
Does she know a lot about the wine business? Why?
Where do her parents live?
Where is her father from?
What are her hobbies/interests?

- We write words like *always/usually/never* after the verb *to be* but before other verbs.

Wordpower   p. 6

1   (Possible answers)
Family: daughter, aunt, married.
Flat/House: lounge, bedroom, garage, kitchen.
Jobs: dentist, firefighter, actor, farmer, secretary, artist.

2   to live in a house/a village/ a town
to work part-time
to go to work by car/by train/by underground
go to the cinema
listen to music
play tennis
read newspapers and magazines
watch TV

3   Interests: cinema, photography, reading, music.
Sports: swimming, walking, tennis.

Skills focus   p. 8

1   1   (Possible answers)
Australia, Canada, New Zealand, South Africa, UK, USA
2   a. about 350 million
3   umbrella   Italian
marmalade   Portuguese
élite   French
quartz   German
cargo   Spanish

Social English   p. 9

1   1   Usually, people in Britain only shake hands when they meet for the first time, or when they meet again after a long time.
2   I'm sorry, I didn't hear your name.
Could you repeat that/say that again, please?
3   *Good morning/Good afternoon/Good evening* are greetings. We say *Goodnight* to say goodbye/end a conversation at night.

2   1   Excuse me, are you...?
May I introduce myself, I'm...
2   How do you do.
3   Let me introduce you to...
I'd like to introduce you to...
Pleased to meet you.

3   1   Excuse me, are you...?
May I introduce myself? I'm...
2   Nice to see you again.
How's the family?
3   I'd like to introduce you to...
Pleased to meet you.

4 How are you? Very well, thank you. And you?
  Pleased to meet you. Pleased to meet you, too.
  How do you do. How do you do.
  Please call me James. Then you must call me Luigi.
  How's life? Not too bad, but very busy.
  Hello, are you Roberto? Yes, that's right.
5 I must go now.
  It was very nice meeting you.
  I look forward to seeing you.
  I really enjoyed meeting you, too.
  Have a good trip back.
  Thank you, and the same to you.

Unit 2

Language focus   p. 10

2 1 A *customer* is a person who buys goods or services, usually from a shop or company.
    A *buyer* is a person whose job is to choose and buy the goods which large shops sell to their customers.
    A *supplier* supplies the goods which shops sell to their customers.
  2 A *collection* is a group of new products, usually of fashion clothes, e.g. *summer fashion collection*.
  3 He sees his secretary, the buyers, and the sales staff.
  4 Yes, he is.
3 1 What does she give him?
  2 Who does he meet?
  3 Who do they visit?/What do they attend?
  4 How often does he walk round his departments?
  5 Who does he talk to?
4 (Possible answer)
  I have a lot of meetings./I'm having a lot of meetings.
  The sentence about Manfred's typical day is in the Present Simple tense. The sentence about Manfred's work this month is in the Present Continuous tense.

  • Use the Present Simple to talk about regular activities, and the Present Continuous to talk about current activities.
  • To make the Present Continuous, use *am/is/are + -ing* form of the verb.

Practice   p. 11

1 1 R   2 R   3 C   4 R   5 C   6 R   7 C   8 C
2 1 works   2 spends   3 phone   4 ask
  5 is speaking   6 is giving   7 enjoys   8 meets
  9 is organizing   10 are making   11 are filming
  12 want
3 Miss Adams   She's giving a presentation to the sales staff.
  Mr Smith   He's visiting our London office.
  Mr Kurtz   He's making a phone call to Paris.
  Mrs Li   She's attending a conference.
  Ms Engel   She's seeing a customer.
  Dr Brown   He's/She's having lunch with a supplier.

Pronunciation   p. 12

1 /pɑːks/   /draɪvz/   /fɪnɪʃɪz/
2 1 drives /z/   3 discusses /ɪz/   5 spends /z/
  2 visits /s/   4 speaks /s/   6 finishes /ɪz/

5 (Possible questions)
  1 When do you start/finish work?
  2 What time/Where do you usually have lunch?
  3 Do you sometimes have a lot of meetings?
  4 How often do you make phone calls in English?
  5 Do you generally make a lot of business trips?
    Are you making any business trips this month?
  6 Do you generally meet many visitors?
    Are you meeting any visitors this month?

7 How many days' holiday do you have each year?
  Where do you go for your holidays?
8 Do you do many training courses?
  Are you doing any courses at the moment?
9 What projects are you working on currently?
10 Do you enjoy your job? Why/Why not?
11 How often do you use a computer?
12 How important is English in your work?

Wordpower   p. 13

1 1 2   2 1 b.   3 1 a.   4 1 b.   5 1 a.   6 3
2 to apply for a job
  to find a job
  He's got a part-time/permanent/temporary/well-paid job.

Skills focus   p. 14

1 a. a/one hundred
  b. a/one hundred and fifty
  c. a/one thousand
  d. three thousand five hundred
  e. twenty thousand
  f. thirty thousand five hundred
  g. a/one million
  h. ten million
2 1 250 kinds of cheese   180 sorts of bread and patisserie   100 tons of chocolate
  2 4,000 years ago
  3 70% of its own electricity   11,500 light bulbs   30,000 customers   300,000 customers
  4 £1.5 million on an average day
  5 £9 million for the first day

Social English   p. 16

1 Message for   Monique Bresson
  Caller's name   James Turner
  Company   *Wine and Dine* magazine
  Number   0171 331 8579
  Please call.
2 Could I speak to Monique Bresson, please?
  Who's calling, please?
  Hold the line, please.
  I'm sorry. She's in a meeting.
  Can I take a message?
  Could you ask her to call me?
4 1 speak   2 calling, please   3 It's   4 the line
5 1 b.   2 b.   3 a.   4 b.
6 /eɪ/ (as in **say**)   a   h   j   k
  /iː/ (as in **she**)   e   b   c   d   g   p   t   v
  /e/ (as in **ten**)   f   l   m   n   s   x   z
  /aɪ/ (as in **fly**)   i   y
  /əʊ/ (as in **go**)   o
  /ɑː/ (as in **bar**)   r
  /uː/ (as in **who**)   u   q   w

Unit 3

Language focus   p. 18

3 Profession   engineer
  Length of stay   twelve days (two-day meeting, ten days in Scotland)
  Places visited   London/Edinburgh/the Scottish Highlands
  Activities   sightseeing/touring/walking in the mountains
4 1 lasted   6 spent   11 didn't have
  2 stayed   7 didn't visit 12 Did,visit
  3 did,stay 8 did,do   13 went
  4 invited   9 saw   14 visited
  5 Did,go   10 ate   15 took

- Use the Past Simple for finished situations and actions in the past.
- To make the negative, use *did + not (didn't)+* infinitive.
- To make the question, use *did +* subject *+* infinitive.

Practice   p. 19

1 eat/ate come/came do/did fly/flew find/found
have/had meet/met say/said see/saw spend/spent
think/thought take/took

Pronunciation   p. 20

1 The *-ed* ending of *visited*, *lasted*, and *attended* is pronounced as an extra syllable, /ɪd/.
2 *watched* /t/   *enjoyed* /d/   *invited* /ɪd/   *toured* /d/
visited /ɪd/   *talked* /t/   *attended* /ɪd/

- In the Past Simple, when the infinitive ends in *d* or *t*, pronounce the *-ed* ending as /ɪd/.

2 1 came   5 rented   9 met
   2 spent/had   6 toured   10 didn't understand
   3 did   7 walked   11 Did, have
   4 visited/saw   8 saw/visited
4 **Group A** (Possible questions)
   What's your name?
   What do you do?
   Did you come to the UK on business?
   How many days did you spend in London?
   Did you visit any interesting places?
   What did you do in the evenings?
   Where did you stay?

Wordpower   p. 22

1 Accommodation: hotel/holiday flat/tent/bed and breakfast/villa
   Travel: plane/coach/train/ferry
   Activities: (beach) sunbathing/swimming/sailing (mountains) climbing/skiing (cities) sightseeing/museums
2 (Possible answers)
   to have a   walking holiday
                  climbing holiday
   to do some   swimming
                  windsurfing
                  sailing/snorkelling
   to go   sightseeing
                  skiing
                  windsurfing
                  hitch-hiking

Skills focus   p. 23

1 (Possible answers)
   network of hotels with conference facilities, wonderful climate, good food and wine, museums and art galleries

Social English   p. 25

1 1 He wants to see Wayne Brown.
   2 She asks him to take a seat.
3 Did you have any problems finding us?
   How was your flight?
4 1 He came to San Francisco as a student, and discovered Californian wines.
   2 He got a job with a wine merchant, then wrote an article for a wine magazine.
5 1, 3, 4, and 5 are important to make a good conversation.
6 James and Wayne do all these things, so their conversation is a good model.

Unit 4

Language focus   p. 26

2 (Possible answers)
   nightlife, beaches, restaurants, museums, cinemas, theatres, good hotels, beautiful buildings, famous sights
4 biggest few largest nearest older oldest
   healthier liveliest loveliest most cosmopolitan
   more enjoyable most exciting more impressive best
   more less

Two-syllable adjectives ending in *-y*
- To make the superlative, change the *-y* to *-i* and add *-est* to the end of the adjective.
Other two-syllable adjectives and three-syllable adjectives
- To make the superlative, put *most* before the adjective.

Practice   p. 28

1   1 easiest   12 longer
    2 widest   13 more peaceful
    3 more crowded   14 most popular
    4 noisier   15 oldest
    5 most beautiful   16 finest
    6 most dangerous   17 more famous
    7 safer   18 best
    8 more suitable   19 fewer
    9 most accessible   20 cheaper
   10 best   21 most exciting
   11 farther (further) 22 most expensive

Pronunciation   p. 29

2 1 a. 2 b.   3 a.   4 b.   5 b.   6 a.
4 1 b. 2 b.   3 a.   4 a.   5 b.   6 a.

2 (Possible answers)
   The USA is bigger than Australia.
   The USA is smaller than Canada.
   The population of Canberra is smaller than the population of Ottawa.
   Australia has the smallest population.
   Washington DC has more citizens than Canberra.
   The population of Australia is lower than the population of Canada.

Wordpower   p. 30

1 (Possible answers)
   a. business trip: conference/meeting rooms, equipment such as computers, OHPs
   b. family holiday: good food, comfortable rooms, swimming-pool, family bar
2 in-room hair dryer 7   cocktail bar 2   restaurant 1
   fitness centre 8   facilities for disabled 5   swimming-pool 4   tennis courts 10   in-room safes 9   conferences and meetings 6   air-conditioning 3
4 8 bath   10 shower   11 tap   1 toilet
   4 shaver socket   6 hair dryer   9 towel
   3 bathrobe   5 soap   7 toothbrush   2 toothpaste

Skills focus   p. 31

1 The company's most successful sales staff.

2

	Hamilton	Heron	Bedarra
General information	largest island, widest choice of activities, nightlife	quieter, more relaxing than Hamilton, national park, birdwatching	smaller, more exclusive
Accommodation	for 1,400 people	for 250 people lower prices	most expensive for 32 people only
Facilities	restaurants, bars, nightclubs, shops	1 restaurant	2 restaurants
Sport	all water sports, tennis, golf	scuba-diving, snorkelling	swimming, windsurfing, sailing, tennis

Social English   p. 32

1 1 James wants to book another room for a colleague for 4 April.
   2 The hotel is fully booked for 4 April.
2 single room
   I'm very sorry
   what a pity
   Thank you for your help
3 I have a reservation.
   Could you fill in this form, please, and sign here?
   Here's your key.
   The porter will take your luggage.
   Could I have an early morning call, at 6.30?
   Do you need anything else?
4 1 False   2 True
5 Could I have   by credit card
   Can I pay   you enjoyed
   we take   very much

Review unit A   p. 34

3 speak English on the phone, play a sport, write letters in English, make business trips, give presentations, work flexitime, read professional literature, attend meetings or conferences
4 1 writes   8 specialize   15 talked
   2 moved   9 is interviewing 16 enjoyed
   3 lives   10 have   17 didn't like
   4 isn't   11 flew   18 loves
   5 spends   12 spent   19 meets
   6 is doing   13 was   20 does she enjoy
   7 is visiting   14 joined   21 likes
5 (Possible questions)
   1 Where did you go?
   2 How long did you go for?
   3 Was it your first holiday in Majorca?
   4 Where did you stay?
   5 Did you like the Spanish food?
   6 What did you do?
   7 What was the weather like?
   8 Did you have any problems?
6 1 fewer, fewest
   2 livelier, liveliest
   3 more crowded, most crowded
   4 better, best
   5 more suitable, most suitable
   6 more, most
   7 farther (further), farthest (furthest)
   8 worse, the worst
   9 more enjoyable, most enjoyable
  10 less, least
  11 bigger, biggest
  12 easier, easiest

9 (Possible answers)
   Could I speak to   isn't here
   's calling   take a message?
   This is   Could you ask him
   the line   I'll give him your message.

Unit 5

Language focus   p. 38

1 (Possible answers)
   People often feel stiff, suffer from jet-lag, tiredness, and headaches after long flights. They can do exercises to reduce tiredness and stiffness during flight. They can try to sleep. They can be careful of what they eat and drink.
2 The programme suggests that travellers don't drink alcohol, tea, or coffee as these can increase jet-lag. They suggest water or juices are better. There is a special menu with light meals. The programme also gives detailed exercises for passengers to prevent stiffness.
3 1 F   2 T   3 F   4 T   5 F
4 1 didn't have any   2 a lot of   3 didn't drink any
   4 any   5 some   6 Not many   7 drank a lot of

Mass and count nouns
Mass   *coffee information alcohol sleep champagne *fruit juice advice luggage
Count *coffee magazine *fruit juice trip plane problem passenger vegetable

• Mass nouns do not have a plural form. We cannot count them.
• Some *nouns are both mass and count.

some and *any*
• Use *any* in negative sentences, and for questions.
• Use *some* and *any* with both mass and count nouns.

a lot of/much/many
• Use *a lot of* with both mass and count nouns in positive sentences.
• Use *much* with mass nouns in negative sentences and in questions.
• Use *many* with count nouns in negative sentences and in questions.

Practice   p. 41

1 1 some   2 any   3 some   4 any   5 some   6 some
   7 any   8 some   9 any   10 some
2 1 a lot of   2 much   3 many   4 a lot of   5 a lot of
   6 many   7 a lot of   8 many

Pronunciation   p. 41

2/3
   1 magazine   •   5 problem •
   2 passenger •   6 cigarette •
   3 exercise •   7 vegetable •
   4 advice •   8 brochure •

Wordpower   p. 42

1

Meat	Poultry	Fish/Seafood	Vegetables	Fruit
pork	chicken	prawns	mushrooms	lemon
veal		trout	potatoes	strawberries
		Dover sole	onions	bananas
			green beans	figs
				passion fruit

3 smoked grilled roast sautéed grilled fried
4 1 grilled   2 fried   3 roast

Skills focus   p. 43

1 1 c. France   2 It reduces the risk of heart attack.
3 beef   4 a. France b. Spain c. Italy d. Greece. They
are all made with garlic.

Social English   p. 44

1 King prawns, smoked salmon, Dover sole, Normandy
pork, a bottle of Sancerre.
2 Monique.
3 (Possible answer) Perhaps James wants to ask Monique
out for dinner to celebrate *her* birthday.
4 **Recommending**
What do you recommend?
The … is usually excellent here.
I recommend…
Ordering
I'll have…
I'd like…
Offering
Do have some more…
How about…?
Would you like…?
Accepting
Yes. That would be very nice.
Declining
Thank you, but I couldn't eat any more.
Thanking and responding
Thank you for a lovely evening.
Don't mention it.
I enjoyed it very much, too.
5 (Possible answers)
do you recommend?
duck pâté
what about veal cutlets?
that would be nice
what would you like
Red wine
I'd like that
how about
I couldn't eat any more
Are you
What about
Yes, I'd like that
for a really excellent meal
Don't mention it

Unit 6

Language focus   p. 46

1 1   The Manager must meet and socialize with a
lot of people, and make presentations.
2 Extract 1=1987 (Diploma)
Extract 2=1987–89 (Assistant Manager)
Extract 3=1990–93 (Manager)
Extract 4=1993–Present (Corporate Client Services
Manager)
3 Erwin uses the Past Simple to talk about his previous
jobs. Those jobs are finished. He uses a *different* tense
(Present Perfect Simple) to talk about his current job.
This job is not finished.

- To make the Present Perfect Simple, use *has* or *have* +
  the past participle of the verb (*travelled, been, increased*).
- Use the Past Simple for finished situations and actions in
  the past.
- Use the Present Perfect Simple for past actions with
  present results.

4 1   For Europe and Japan.
2   Yes, she spent a month there in 1993.
3   Yes, a lot.
4   No.

Practice   p. 50

1

Past Simple	Past Participle
bought	bought
did	done
ate	eaten
gave	given
went	gone/been
made	made
met	met
read	read
saw	seen
wrote	written

2 **Student A**
1   Have you had a holiday this year?
2   Have you bought anything expensive recently?
3   Have you made any business trips in the last three
months?
4   Have you done any sport this week?
5   Have you met any foreigners this month?
Student B
1   Have you eaten any foreign food recently?
2   Have you written any letters this week?
3   Have you had a birthday in the last six months?
4   Have you seen any good films this month?
5   Have you read any good books recently?
3 1 has travelled   2 has made   3 has visited
4 spent   5 met   6 has given   7 has produced
8 has never travelled   9 travelled   10 was

Pronunciation   p. 51

2 1 a.   2 b.   3 b.   4 a.   5 a.   6 a.   7 b.   8 b.

---

4 1   Have you (ever) worked in the tourist industry?
2   Have you (ever) done any marketing or sales?
3   Have you (ever) given any presentations?
4   Have you (ever) studied any European languages?
5   Have you (ever) travelled on a luxury train?
6   Have you (ever) been on a cruise?
7   Have you (ever) organized a conference or other
corporate activity?
8   Have you (ever) wanted to work in the luxury travel
industry?

Wordpower   p. 52

1 Job advertisement: job title, salary, working conditions.
CV: personal details, experience, qualifications. Short list:
interview, candidate.
2 1   job vacancy   9   curriculum vitae
2   advertisement   10   personal details
3   job title   11   experience
4   job requirements   12   short list
5   salary   13   interview
6   working conditions 14   candidate
7   career prospects   15   appointment
8   application

3

Verb	Activity	Person 1	Person 2
employ	employment	employer	employee
interview	interview	interviewer	interviewee
train	training	trainer	trainee

Skills focus   p. 53

2 2   Find out about the interviewer or interviewers.
3   Make a checklist of questions to ask at interview.
5   Arrive in good time.
6   Create a good first impression.
8   Don't give only 'Yes' or 'No' answers.
9   Ask questions.
10   Learn from the interview.

Social English   p. 54

1 (Possible answer)
  Duncan is writing to invite Monique to lunch to discuss business with her.

2 Lunch with Duncan Ross, Tuesday, 1.30 p.m. at Claret's restaurant.

3 **Making an appointment**
  When would be convenient for you?
  Is...possible for you?
  Shall we say...
  What time would suit you?
  How about...?
  Saying 'yes'
  Yes, that's fine.
  I look forward to meeting you...

4 1 She can't come to the meeting on Tuesday.
  2 No, he has another appointment then.
  3 Friday 18th.

5 **Making an appointment**
  When are you free?
  Is... possible for you?
  What about...?
  Saying 'yes'
  Yes. I can make it on...
  See you on...
  Saying 'no'
  No, I'm afraid I've got another appointment...
  Changing an appointment
  I'm very sorry.
  I'm afraid I can't manage our meeting on...
  Could we arrange another time?

6 (Possible answers)
  Chris
  Andrew
  What time would be convenient
  How about
  I'm afraid I'm busy
  What about
  that suits me fine
  Shall we say
  Yes, that's fine

8 (Possible answers)
  Jan
  speaking
  Armand
  I have to cancel our meeting on Saturday.
  arrange another time
  that's fine
  are you free
  Monday convenient
  I'm afraid I have another appointment then.
  Tuesday
  that's fine
  See you on Tuesday at 9 a.m.

Unit 7

Language focus   p. 56

2 British
  Florence/Italy
  designer
  designer for Ferragamo
  freelance designer
  It's easier and more interesting to work as a designer in Italy.

3 The tenses are the Present Simple, Past Simple, the Present Perfect Simple, and the Present Perfect Continuous.

- Use the Present Perfect Simple for past actions in a time period up to the present when we give the quantity.
- To make the Present Perfect Continuous, use *has/have + been + -ing* form of the verb.
- Use the Present Perfect Continuous for an action that began in the past and continues to the present.

Practice   p. 57

1 (Possible answers)
  1 has been working   4 has travelled
  2 has made   5 has made
  3 has been designing

- Use *since* with a point of time and *for* with a length of time.

2 1 for   2 for   3 since   4 since   5 since   6 since
  7 for   8 since   9 for   10 since

3 1 have been   2 have been growing   3 have become
  4 have made   5 started   6 has increased
  7 has grown

Pronunciation   p. 59

1 Listener b. sounds more interested.
2 1, 3, 4, and 5.

Wordpower   p. 60

1 1 to go up, to increase   2 to remain stable
  3 to level off   4 to go down, to decrease, to fall
  5 to reach a peak   6 to improve

2 **Verb**   **Noun**
  Infinitive   **Past**
  to decrease   decreased   a decrease
  to fall   fell   a fall
  to increase   increased   an increase
  to rise   rose   a rise
  to improve   improved   an improvement

3 dramatic/dramatically   sudden, very large
  sharp/sharply   sudden, large
  steady/steadily   regular (not sudden)
  slight/slightly   very small

4 1 by   2 at   3 from, to   4 of   5 in

5 1 increased/rose/went up   2 increase/rise
  3 reached a peak   4 sharply   5 fall/decrease
  6 fell/decreased/went down

Skills focus   p. 62

1 1 Milan   2 400   3 surplus

2 | A | Total value | $30b | D | Germany | 23.1% |
  |---|---|---|---|---|---|
  | B | Germany | 94.5m | | France | 11.4% |
  | | France | 48.2m | | USA | 9.8% |
  | | USA | 29.7m | E | Italy | $6b |
  | C | Asia | 60.4% | | Germany | $5.6b |
  | | W Europe | 11.9% | | UK | $3.7b |
  | | E Europe | 11.2% | | France | $3.3b |

Social English   p. 64

1 1 The tenth anniversary of *Wine and Dine* magazine.
  2 Because Scotland is too far for people to travel.
  3 The publication of James's book on Italian wines.
  4 He thinks it's a wonderful idea.

2 **Asking for opinions**
  What do you think about...?
  What's your opinion of...?
  How do you feel about...?
  Giving opinions
  In my opinion...
  I think...
  Agreeing
  I agree.
  I certainly agree with that.

3 1 T   2 F   3 F   4 T

4 **Making suggestions**
I suggest…
How about…?
Why don't we…?
Why not…?
We could…
Asking for suggestions
Do you have any suggestions for…?
Accepting suggestions
Yes, let's do that.
Rejecting suggestions
I'm not sure about that.

5 (Possible answers)
I suggest we go skiing next weekend.
How about buying tickets for the music festival?
What about going away for a few days?
Why don't we invite some friends for dinner?
Why not spend next Sunday in the country?
We could go to a restaurant in the evening.

▌Unit 8

Language focus   p. 66

1 (Possible answers)
restaurants, bars, sports facilities, laundry services,
business centre with computers, fax, e-mail, photocopier,
etc.

4 1 No, he's arriving by helicopter.
2 In the Conference Room on the first floor.
3 In the garden.
4 No, he isn't.

5 1 flight
2 the President's arrival
3 business facilities
4 business people
5 Roof Garden, Oriental cuisine

- Use the Present Continuous for fixed future arrangements.
- Use *going to* for future plans, intentions, and decisions.

Practice   p. 68

1 1 I'm arriving   4 I'm interviewing
2 I'm travelling   5 I'm spending
3 I'm having

2 (Possible answers)
21 July – he's going on a sightseeing tour of the city.
22 July – he's having dinner with Kiki Johns.
23 July – he's meeting exporters at the Trade Centre.

Pronunciation   p. 69

1 The strong form is in sentence a.
2 1 b. 2 b. 3 a. 4 b. 5 b. 6 a.

- Use the strong form of *to* when the word is at the end of a sentence.

Wordpower   p. 72

1 Terminal: passport control, duty-free shop, security
check, arrivals board, customs, information desk.
Luggage: briefcase, suitcase, trolley. Documents: ticket,
boarding card. On board: overhead locker, seat-belt, life-
jacket, window seat, flight attendant.

Skills focus   p. 73

1
Flight	Airline	Nationality
AF 645	Air France	French
AZ 1420	Alitalia	Italian
MA 732	Malev	Hungarian
LH 4980	Lufthansa	German
IB 3765	Iberia	Spanish
OA 287	Olympic	Greek

2 1 P 2 C 3 P 4 C/A 5 C/A 6 A 7 C 8 A

3
Flight No.	Time	Destination	Information	Gate
AF 962	11.15	Marseilles	Boarding	11
LH 4037	11.25	Dusseldorf	Boarding	28
IB 3915	11.50	Malaga	Delayed	10
AZ 287	11.45	Venice	Last call	15
OA 259	11.45	Athens	Last call	19

4 1 b. 2 a. 3 d. 4 c. 5 e.
5 1 d. 2 b. 3 f. 4 a. 5 c. 6 e.
7 1 shortly 2 are required to 3 remain seated
4 in the upright position 5 to fill in 6 has come to
a complete standstill

Social English   p. 75

1 1 He invites Monique to stay at Glencross after the
celebration.
2 She agrees to stay.
2 1 Because he's going to be very busy.
2 Duncan tells him that Monique is going to stay.
3 **Inviting**
I'd like to invite you to…
Would you join us…?
Would you like to…?
How about…?
Accepting
Thank you. I'd be delighted to accept.
Thank you. I'd love to.
Declining
I'd love to, but (*I'm afraid I can't*).

▌Review unit B   p. 76

1 2, 3, 5, 6, and 9 are correct.
1 Could you give me some information, please?
4 He gave me some useful advice.
7 How much money did you spend?
8 I haven't got any paper.
10 He has a lot of experience in marketing.

3 **Student A**
1 Have you ever been…?
2 Have you ever had…?
3 Have you ever missed…?
4 Have you ever worked…?
5 Have you ever lost…?
Student B
1 Have you ever been…?
2 Have you ever had…?
3 Have you ever studied or worked…?
4 Have you ever met…?
5 Have you ever wanted…?

4 1 I haven't seen him for ages.
2 How long ago did you have a holiday?
3 How long have they been married?
4 I've had my present job for a long time.
5 Have you ever been to Canada?
6 How many candidates have you interviewed today?
7 She changed her job a month ago.
8 How long have you been working for your present
company?
9 He changed jobs twice last year.
10 She's studied Japanese since 1993.

5 1 has been 2 left 3 joined 4 has worked
5 travels 6 was 7 went 8 hasn't been 9 is
10 is 11 have never visited 12 flew
13 have visited

6 1 You've drunk 2 We've been drinking 3 She's
typed, I've signed 4 He's played 5 They've been
walking 6 She's lost, She's been looking

Unit 9

Language focus   p. 80

2 1 It's a proposal for a high-speed European train network.
   2 In 1981.
   3 On many routes, the airlines have lost up to 90% of their passengers to the trains.

3 (Possible answers)
   will revolutionize   will take   will be   'll choose   'll find

- Use *will* + infinitive to predict future situations and actions.
- To make the 1st Conditional, use *if* + the Present Simple, + *will* + infinitive.
- Use the 1st Conditional to express a future possibility and its result.
- Use *if* to express a possibility, and *when* to express a certainty.

Practice   p. 82

1 (Possible answers)
   1 How long will train journeys between major cities take?
   2 How long will the journey from Brussels to Paris take?
   3 How many types of line will there be?
   4 Which method of travel will business people choose?
   5 What will the 21st century be?

Pronunciation   p. 82

2 1 a.   2 b.   3 a.   4 b.   5 b.   6 b.   7 a.   8 a.

Wordpower   p. 85

1 1 Information
   2 Left luggage
   3 Tickets
   4 Lost property
   5 Waiting room
   6 Platforms 1–3
   7 Departures
   8 Buffet
   9 Customer services
2 train/plane/taxi fare
   day return/period return ticket
   monthly/annual season ticket
   underground/intercity trains
3 to catch/miss a plane/a bus
   to drive a train/a bus/a coach/a car/a taxi
   to ride a bicycle/a motorbike
   to get on/off a plane/a train/a bus/a bicycle/a motorbike
   to get into/out of a car/a taxi
   to take a plane/a train/a bus/a coach/a taxi

Skills focus   p. 86

2 (Possible answers)
   1 Because you simply write on it with a pen.
   2 By phone, fax, or by electronic mail.
   3 Yes.

Social English   p. 88

1 Book flight   Edinburgh – Paris on Sunday afternoon/evening
   Book hotel   Paris – three nights
   Get information about   plane and train to Bordeaux on Wednesday
2 1 By direct flight from Bordeaux.
   2 Because he's going to stay with some friends.

3 Requesting   Agreeing
   Can you...?   Yes, of course.
   Could you...?   Yes, certainly.
   Would you mind...
     (+ -ing)?   No, of course not.
   Do you think you
     could...?
   Offering   **Accepting**
   Shall I...?   Yes, please.
   Would you like me   Thank you. I'd appreciate
     to...?   that.
   Do you want me to...?   **Declining**
                             Thanks, but that won't be necessary.

Unit 10

Language focus   p. 90

2 (Possible answers)
   not enough parking spaces
   traffic jams
   inadequate metro system
   too many cars
   double parking/streets blocked by parked cars
   pollution
   health problems
3 a. Caller 3   c. Caller 1
   b. Caller 2   d. Caller 4
4 1 T   2 T   3 F   4 T

- To make the 2nd Conditional, use *if* + Past Simple, + *would* or *could* + infinitive.

Pronunciation   p. 92

1 a. I'd do more <u>sport</u> if I had enough <u>time</u>.
   b. If I earned more <u>money</u>, I'd buy a new <u>car</u>.
2 1 If I had a <u>car</u>, I'd drive it to <u>work</u>.
   2 If I lived in the <u>city</u>, I'd travel by <u>bike</u>.
   3 I'd take more <u>exercise</u> if I were <u>you</u>.
   4 If they banned all <u>cars</u>, the air would be <u>cleaner</u>.
   5 If the buses were <u>quicker</u>, more people would <u>use</u> them.
   6 Would you take the <u>train</u> if you <u>could</u>?

Wordpower   p. 93

1 9 ashtray   12 diary   14 phone   10 bookcase
   18 filing cabinet   3 table lamp   2 chair   1 table
   4 desk   11 clock   17 keyboard   5 photocopier
   13 bin   6 coffee machine   15 year planner
   7 computer   16 mouse   8 mineral water

Skills focus   p. 94

1 1 T   2 F   3 T   4 F   5 F   6 T   7 T   8 T
2 1 We have pleasure in enclosing...
   2 Please contact us again if you would like any further information.
   3 With reference to...
   4 Unfortunately,...
3 1 c.   2 e.   3 a.   4 d.   5 i.   6 b.   7 h.
   8 g.   9 j.   10 f.

Social English   p. 96

1 Flight times

	Edinburgh	Paris
Sun p.m.	14.45	18.45
	16.00	20.50
	18.00	23.05
	Bordeaux	London
Fri p.m.	14.40	15.10

2 Asking for information

I'd like some information about…
Do you know…?
Could you tell me…?

Showing understanding
Right, I've got that.

Checking
Let me check.
I'll look that up.

Apologizing
I'm afraid I don't have any information about…

Asking for repetition
Could you repeat that, please?

3 | Train times | Paris | Bordeaux |
Wed arrive by 1 p.m. 10 a.m. 1 p.m.
Which station? Paris Montparnasse

4 1 Can you tell me when you want to travel?
2 Could you tell me when it leaves?
3 Do you know which station it leaves from?

5 An indirect question is more polite.
In an indirect question, there is no inversion of the subject and verb and no auxiliary verb form, e.g. *do*, *does*, *did*.

6 1 and 3 are correct.
2 I'd like to know how long the journey takes.
4 Can you tell me which airport the flight leaves from?
5 Do you know how much the fare is?
6 I'd like to know where I can buy a ticket.

▌Unit 11

Language focus   p. 98

3 | Topic | Extract 1 | Extract 2 | Extract 3 |
| --- | --- | --- | --- |
| Shaking hands | ✓ | | |
| First/family name | ✓ | ✓ | |
| Titles | | ✓ | |
| Business lunches | ✓ | | |
| Punctuality | | ✓ | |
| Humour and jokes | | ✓ | |
| Business cards | | ✓ | ✓ |
| Making decisions | | | ✓ |
| Invitations | ✓ | ✓ | ✓ |

4 Extract 1   France
Extract 2   Germany
Extract 3   Japan

5 *Must* and *mustn't* offer the strongest advice.

- Use *should/shouldn't* to give advice.
- Use *mustn't* to express a necessity not to do something.
- Use *needn't* to express no necessity to do something.
- Use *may* and *might* to express possibility.
- Use modal verbs without *to* before the infinitive.
- To make the negative, add *not* (*-n't*) to the end of modal verbs.

Practice   p. 100

1 | A | B |
| --- | --- |
| must | it's 100% necessary |
| mustn't | it's 100% necessary not to do it |
| needn't | it's not necessary |
| should | it's a good idea |
| shouldn't | it's a bad idea |
| may | it's about 50% possible |
| might | it's less than 50% possible |

2 1 may/might   2 must   3 should   4 may/might
5 mustn't   6 shouldn't   7 needn't

Pronunciation   p. 101

1 a. mustn't   b. papers
2 1 You <u>might</u> need an umbrella.
2 You <u>should</u> take some <u>cash</u>.
3 You <u>must</u> wear a tie.
4 You <u>shouldn't</u> smoke in here.
5 You <u>mustn't</u> ask for <u>credit</u>.
6 You <u>needn't</u> do it <u>today</u>.

Wordpower   p. 102

1 1 punctual   2 polite   3 sociable   4 honest
5 flexible   6 sincere   7 patient   8 efficient
9 agreeable   10 ambitious

2 | un | in | im | dis |
| --- | --- | --- | --- |
| unpunctual | insincere | impolite | dishonest |
| unsociable | inflexible | impatient | disagreeable |
| unambitious | | | |

4 | polite | politeness | efficient | efficiency |
| --- | --- | --- | --- |
| ambitious | ambition | honest | honesty |
| punctual | punctuality | patient | patience |

Skills focus   p. 103

1 1 a. Italians, Greeks, Spanish, and Portuguese.
b. Swedes, Finns, Norwegians, and Danes.
2 North Europeans seem to need more personal space than south Europeans.
3 It seems to be more acceptable to stare at people in Mediterranean countries than in some other countries in Europe.

Social English   p. 105

1 (Possible answers)
1 It doesn't matter./Don't worry.
2 Don't mention it./Not at all.
3 Thanks, and the same to you.
4 Please do./Well, I'd rather you didn't.

3 1 b.   2 a.   3 a.   4 b.   5 b.   6 a.   7 b.   8 a.

5 1 Can I get you another drink?   e. Thanks. I'll have a whisky.
2 Sorry, I've spilt some wine.   d. It doesn't matter.
3 Thank you for all your help.   f. Don't mention it.
4 You live in France, don't you?   c. Yes, that's right.
5 Do you mind if I smoke?   g. Well, I'd rather you didn't.
6 He's a millionaire, you know.   a. Really!
7 I lost the tennis match.   i. Never mind. Better luck next time.
8 May I join you?   b. Please do.
9 Could you pass the ice, please?   h. Yes, here you are.
10 Is this your first visit to Glencross?   j. No, I've been here before.

7 1 ✓   2 ✓   4 ✓   6 ✓   8 ✓

▌Unit 12

Language focus   p. 106

1 Napoleon said 'In victory you deserve it. In defeat you need it.'

2 1 Only sparkling wine which is produced in the Champagne area of France.
2 The wine is 'le champagne'. The region is 'la Champagne'.
3 No, it's made from two varieties of black grape, Pinot Noir and Pinot Meunier, and one white grape, Chardonnay. 'Blanc de Blancs' champagne is made from white grapes only.

138 ☞ **ANSWER KEY**

4   200 kilometres of chalk cellars.
5   The Benedictine monk who developed the 'méthode champenoise' in the 17th century.
6   Vintage champagne is produced from the grapes of the same year. Non-vintage champagne is made by blending the wine reserves of different years.

3   (Possible answers)
is produced (Present Simple)   was made (Past Simple)
are used (Present Simple)   have been used (Present Perfect Simple)   has been produced (Present Perfect Simple)

> • To make the passive, use the verb *to be* in the correct tense + the past participle of the verb (e.g. *made*, *produced*, *grown*).
> • Use the passive when you want to describe actions without describing who does them.
> • When we want to say who does the action in a passive sentence, we use the word *by*.

Practice   p. 108

1
1	are picked	8	is bottled	15	is removed
2	are used	9	are produced	16	are added
3	are pressed	10	is produced	17	is left
4	are used	11	is removed	18	are labelled
5	is left	12	is carried out	19	are inserted
6	are blended	13	are turned	20	is sold
7	are added	14	is frozen		

2   (Possible questions)
1   How long have vines been grown in the Champagne area of France?
2   When was champagne first made?
3   What is champagne made from?
4   How is 'Blanc de Blancs' champagne made?
5   How long have the chalk cellars been used?
6   How many days of sun are needed for a vintage year?
7   How is non-vintage champagne made?

3   1 has been exported   2 was sold   3 were lost
4 was solved   5 was introduced   6 was produced
7 were hit   8 was imported   9 is sold
10 is called

Wordpower   p. 112

1   1   slump, recession
2   decade
3   boom
4   No. In the first headline *cut* is a verb. In the second, *cuts* is a noun.
5   Yes, it's good for export markets.
6   No. People are buying more.

2
Verb	Noun (activity)	Noun (person)
compete	competition	competitor
consume	consumption	consumer
export	exporting	exporter
manufacture	manufacturing	manufacturer
produce	production	producer
recover	recovery	

Pronunciation   p. 112

3   consumption: financial, domestic
recovery: Australian, appreciate
marketing: passenger, traveller
competition: occupation, invitation
5   pronunciation   celebration   manager   programmer
expedition   exhibition   corporation   computer

Skills focus   p. 113

2   1   1980s – 'boom years'

	Year	No. of bottles
Highest sales	1989	249 million
Highest production level	1990	293 million

2   Decline in market since 80s
Main reasons
1   the recession in champagne's export markets
2   the very high price of champagne
3   there was a lot of 'bad' champagne on the market

3
Price of grapes (per kilo)	Today	In 1990
	20 French francs	36 French francs

4   Market in future
Increase in sales?   Yes, when economic situation improves.
Aim of changes   To make sure producers meet very high standards.

Social English   p. 115

1   Dialogue 1
1   To stay with them in Bordeaux.
2   Yes, he has.
Dialogue 2
1   To stay at Glencross Castle again.
2   In London on the 22nd.
(Possible answers)
Dialogue 3
1   Another book.
2   Because he thinks their meeting is social or romantic.
3   Because other men find Monique attractive.

2
Thanking for hospitality	Positive comment
Thank you for inviting us.	We've had a wonderful time.
Thank you very much for your hospitality.	I really appreciated it.
Thanks a lot.	Everything was great.

Responding to thanks
I'm glad you enjoyed it.
Saying goodbye
We really must leave now.
I must be off.
I'm looking forward to…
See you next week.
Have a good flight.
See you… on the…

4   1 d.   2 c.   3 a.   4 b.

Review unit C   p. 116

3   1   mustn't   3   needn't   5   must
2   must   4   mustn't   6   needn't
4   1 h.   2 e.   3 f.   4 a.   5 g.   6 b.   7 c.   8 d.
6   1 was introduced   2 was added   3 was made   4 was drunk   5 was opened   6 has been produced   7 has been developed   8 is consumed   9 is eaten
8   1   Could you tell me what the plane fare from Barcelona to Paris is?
2   Do you know how long the flight takes?
3   Can you tell me which airport in Paris the plane arrives at?
4   Could you tell me when I need to check in?
5   Do you know if I can buy duty-free goods on the plane?
9   1 c.   2 e.   3 f.   4 g.   5 h.   6 a.   7 b.   8 d.

Oxford University Press, Great Clarendon Street, Oxford OX2 6DP

Oxford New York

Athens Auckland Bangkok Bogota Bombay Buenos Aires
Calcutta Cape Town Dar es Salaam Delhi Florence Hong Kong
Istanbul Karachi Kuala Lumpur Madras Madrid Melbourne
Mexico City Nairobi Paris Singapore Taipei Tokyo Toronto Warsaw

and associated companies in
Berlin Ibadan

OXFORD and OXFORD ENGLISH
are trade marks of Oxford University Press

ISBN 0 19 435650 7

© Oxford University Press 1996

First published 1996
Third impression 1998

No unauthorized photocopying

ACKNOWLEDGEMENTS

**The author would like to thank Tracy Byrne for her feedback on the
complete manuscript, and all the staff at Oxford University Press for
their invaluable help in producing this book. The author would also like
to thank Kevin McNicholas for his contributions to the pronunciation
sections of this book.**

**The author and publishers are grateful to the following readers for giving
so much of their time and professional expertise to this project:**
Imogen Arnold
Gillian Brown
Tim Falla
Patsy Fuller
Bridget Green
Jon Hird
Heather Jones
Frances Lowndes
Kevin McNicholas
Mike Macfarlane
Peter Watkins
Angela Winkler

**The publishers and author are grateful to the following individuals and
institutions for helping with research, for piloting sample units, and for
providing invaluable comment and feedback on the manuscript:**
Lynn Andrews
Mark Baker
Gillian Carless
Lynette Dennerstein
Margaret Fowler
Simon Gardner
John Golding
Judy Guttridge
Sue Harrand
Veronica Houghton
Vered Jerome
Aneta Janiszewska
Hanna Kryszewska
Caroline Labaeye
Michael Levene
Debby Liddiatt
David Massey
Penny McLarty
Jane McKinlay
Cristina Nogueira
Eliane Paim
Eloise Price
Sasha Sandford
Cathy Schilbach
Roy Sprenger
Sue Steel
Margaret Stewart
Monika Szabó
Esther Timár

British Institute, Milan/Rome
Cetradel, France
Citylangues, Paris
Chambre de Commerce, France
Culturas Inglesas, Brazil
International House, London
Linguarama, Milan
Linguarama, Barcelona
Lublin Business School, Poland

Illustrations by:
Stefan Chabluk pages 62, 83, 114
Madeleine David page 33
Oliver Hutton page 87
Alan Nanson page 81
Mike Ritchie page 47
Jane Spencer page 28
OUP Technical Graphics Department page 39

Alex Tiani pages 9, 25, 38, 53, 65, 84, 89, 91, 98, 100, 102, 105, 116, 118
Martin Ursell pages 31, 43
Emma Whiting pages 3, 7

Location photography by:
Philip Dunn pages 1, 2, 4, 5, 9, 16, 19, 25, 32, 44, 48, 49, 64, 75, 88, 96, 115
Rob Judges page 85
Stephen Oliver pages 30, 93

Studio photography by:
Stephen Oliver pages 13, 15, 21, 31, 38, 101, 106

**The Publishers would like to thank the following for their kind
permission to reproduce photographs and other copyright material:**
Aquarius Picture Library page 65
Apple Computer (U.K.) Limited pages 86, 87, for extracts from publicity
leaflet 'Your World, Your Newton', and for recorded briefing.
Arcaid page 74 (D Gilbert: *Osaka airport*)
The Austrian National Tourist Office (ANTO) for extracts from information
guide to Vienna.
BMP DDB Needham page 23 (*opening ceremony*)
British Airways page 38 (*food* and *face spray*)
British Airways and Premier Magazines for extracts from *High Life* in-flight
magazine.
Burberrys page 56
J Allan Cash Photo Library page 26 (*waterfront*)
Cephas Picture Library pages 43 (M Rock), 106 (M Rock: *Chardonnay
grapes*), 108 (M Rock: *harvesting grapes, levelling, racking* and *remuage*)
Colorsport pages 23 (S Fraser: *fireworks*), 24 (A Cowie: *F Rouiz*)
Comstock pages 18 (*Rio*), 20, 26 (N Hall: *bridge*), 28 (*Bondi beach*), 36, 47,
55, 66 (*dining room* and *business centre*), 67, 70 (*St Stephen's*), 71 (*church*
and *cafe*), 72 (*check-in* and *passport control*), 78 (*man*), 90 (*Berlin*), 104 (*man
and woman*), 106 (*Pinot Noir grapes*), 117
Eye Ubiquitous page 104 (G Wickham: *Cuban boys*)
Food Features/Steve Moss page 42
Groupe Danone for extracts from publicity leaflet page 114
Robert Harding Photo Library pages 10 (*El Corte Ingles*, A Williams:
Harrods, N Francis: *Bloomingdales*), 31 (*Hamilton Island*), 39 (G Genin:
Jumbo), 45 (A Woolfitt), 70 (*Big wheel*, A Woolfitt: *Belvedere*, P Craven:
Shonbrunn), 71 (D Kay: *Heurigan*), 72 (P van Riel: *baggage reclaim*), 76
(*Waldkirch: industry*, A Woolfitt: *trams*), 78 (*woman*)
Harrods, Knightsbridge, for use of their logo and recorded interviews page 14
Hulton Deutch Library page 74 (*passengers 1933* and *passengers wave goodbye*)
Hutchinson Picture Library pages 66 (R I Cloyd: *hotel room*), 104 (J Horner:
French confectioners)
Ikea Ltd, for extracts from catalogue and use of their logo page 15
The Image Bank page 103 (M Tcherevkoff)
Images pages 18 (*Venice*), 39 (*New York*)
Impact page 28 (N Morrison: *surfer*)
International Coffee Organisation for extracts from the 'Coffee Story'.
International Union of Railways for adapted map.
Life File pages 26 (E Lee: *Opera House*), 71 (E Lee: *Hundertwasser House*, E
Tan: *Uno City*)
Milepost 9 1/2 Library pages 46, 97 (*SNCF*)
Oxford University Press for extract from *Oxford Dictionary of Business
English*, ed. Allene Tuck, © OUP 1993, and extract from *Oxford Wordpower
Dictionary*, ed. Sally Wehmeier, © OUP 1993.
Janet Price page 113
Quadrant Picture Library pages 74 (*cabin 1945* and *airline food 1953*), 80
(Milliken: *electric loco, Rome*, D and M: *TGV*, A Dalton: *ICE*)
SATRA Footwear Technology Centre for chart from ICERES (Shoe Industry
Report).
SOA Library pages 56 (A Simms: *Armani*), 58 (A Simms: *Lauren*)
Spanish National Tourist Office for use of their logo.
Susan Hill page 56
Swatch SA, Zurich & Biel, for extracts from catalogue and use of their logo
page 15
The Telegraph Colour Library pages 10 (*businessman*), 81
Tony Stone Images pages 8 (E Honowitz), 23 (S Powell: *flag*), 24 (C Ehlers:
Expo 92), 28 (S&N Geary: *Palm beach, vineyard*), 64 (M Leman: *castle*), 66
(T Brown: *gym*), 90 (E Pritchard: *Bangkok*), 99 (T Brown)
Travel Ink Library page 76 (D Toase: *gardens*)
The Travel Library pages 18 (*Bath, Paris*), 76 (P Enticknap: *Rome*), 97 (*plane*)
Trip pages 23 (H Rogers: *monorail*), 24 (H Rogers: *pavillion*) 31 (E Smith:
Heron Island, D Saunders: *Heron Island*), 31 (D Saunders), 35 (D Saunders:
Safari, Zebras/Giraffes), 72 (N Price: *plane interior*), 104 (*Man in dish dash*),
106 (J Highet: *Champagne bottles*), 108 (J Highet: *dressing up*)
Vinexpo, the International wine and spirits exhibition, for use of their logo page 2
Yves Saint Laurent page 56 (D Seidner)

**We would also like to thank the following for their help and
co-operation:**
Giorgio Armani
British Airways
B&Q, Swindon
British Telecom
Debenhams PLC
The Manager and staff of the Feathers Hotel, Woodstock
Air France
Grape Ideas, Oxford
Hampden House, Great Missenden
Heathrow Airport
Oddbins, Little Clarendon St., Oxford
Salisburys, Oxford

**The author and publisher would like to thank the following individuals
for agreeing to be be interviewed for this book:**
Clive Girling
Susan Hill
Freddy Price
Peter Willasey
Manfred Zipp